Strategy
and the
Business Landscape

Core Concepts

Pankaj Ghemawat

with

David J. Collis

Gary P. Pisano

Jan W. Rivkin

Prentice
Hall

Upper Saddle River, New Jersey 07458

Library of Congress Cataloging-in-Publication Date

Strategy and the business landscape. Core concepts/Pankaj Ghemawat—1st ed.
   p. cm.
  Includes index.
  ISBN 0–13–028976–0
  1. Strategic planning. 2. Industrial management. I. Ghemawat, Pankaj.

HD30.28.S73967 2000
658.4'012—dc21   00–032629

Senior Editor: David Shafer
Managing Editor (Editorial): Jennifer Glennon
Editorial Assistant: Kim Marsden
Assistant Editor: Michele Foresta
Media Project Manager: Michele Faranda
Senior Marketing Manager: Michael Campbell
Managing Editor (Production): Judy Leale
Production Editor: Emma Moore
Permissions Coordinator: Suzanne Grappi
Production Assistant: Keri Jean
Associate Director, Manufacturing: Vincent Scelta
Production Manager: Paul Smolenski
Design Manager: Patricia Smythe
Cover Design: Michael Fruhbeis
Cover Art/Photo: Photo Researchers Inc./Spencer Grant
Associate Director, Multimedia Production: Karen Goldsmith
Manager, Print Production: Christy Mahon

10 9 8 7 6 5 4 3
ISBN 0–13–028976–0

Dedication

To my colleagues and students

About the Author

Pankaj Ghemawat is the Jaime and Josefina Chu Tiampo Professor of Business Administration at Harvard University's Graduate School of Business Administration. After receiving his Ph.D. in Business Economics from Harvard University, he worked as a consultant with McKinsey & Company in London during 1982 and 1983, and has taught at the Harvard Business School since then. In 1991, Professor Ghemawat was appointed the youngest full professor in the Business School's history. Between 1995 and 1998, he headed its required first-year course on Competition and Strategy.

Professor Ghemawat's other publications include *Commitment* (Free Press, 1991) and *Games Businesses Play* (MIT Press, 1997) as well as several dozen articles and case studies. He currently serves as the Chair of Harvard University's Ph.D. program in Business Economics and on the editorial boards of the *Journal of Economics and Management Strategy*, *Strategic Management Journal*, and *Journal of Management and Governance*.

Contents

C H A P T E R *1*

The Origins of Strategy   1

BACKGROUND   2

ACADEMIC UNDERPINNINGS   4

THE RISE OF STRATEGY CONSULTANTS   8
  BCG and the Experience Curve   9
  From the Experience Curve to Portfolio Analysis   9
  Strategic Business Units and Portfolio Analysis   10

EMERGING PROBLEMS   13

C H A P T E R *2*

Mapping the Business Landscape   19

Pankaj Ghemawat and David J. Collis

SUPPLY-DEMAND ANALYSIS   21

THE "FIVE FORCES" FRAMEWORK   24
  Force 1: The Degree of Rivalry   25
  Force 2: The Threat of Entry   28
  Force 3: The Threat of Substitutes   29
  Force 4: Buyer Power   30
  Force 5: Supplier Power   31

THE VALUE NET AND OTHER GENERALIZATIONS   31

THE PROCESS OF MAPPING BUSINESS LANDSCAPES   35
  Step 1: Drawing the Boundaries   35
  Step 2: Mapping Key Relationships   38
  Step 3: Adapting to/Shaping the Business Landscape   43

C H A P T E R *3*

Creating Competitive Advantage   49

Pankaj Ghemawat and Jan W. Rivkin

THE DEVELOPMENT OF CONCEPTS FOR COMPETITIVE POSITIONING   51
    Cost Analysis   52
    Differentiation Analysis   53
    Costs Versus Differentiation   54
    Added Value   58

A PROCESS FOR ANALYSIS   60
    Step 1: Using Activities to Analyze Relative Costs   62
    Step 2: Using Activities to Analyze Relative Willingness
       to Pay   65
    Step 3: Exploring Different Strategic Options and
       Making Choices   68

THE WHOLE VERSUS THE PARTS   70

C H A P T E R *4*

Anticipating Competitive and Cooperative Dynamics   75

COMPETITION AND COOPERATION AMONG THE FEW   75
    Game Theory   76
    Behavioral Theory   79

EVOLUTIONARY DYNAMICS   81

THREATS TO ADDED VALUE   84
    Imitation   84
    Substitution   90

THREATS TO THE APPROPRIABILITY OF ADDED VALUE   95
    Holdup   95
    Slack   101

CHAPTER *5*

Building and Sustaining Success   111

Pankaj Ghemawat and Gary P. Pisano

ACTIVITIES VERSUS RESOURCES   112
   The Activity-System View   113
   The Resource-Based View   116

DYNAMIC THEORIES   119
   Making Commitments   121
   Developing Capabilities   124

THE CHALLENGE OF CHANGE   127

CREDITS   135

NAME INDEX   137

COMPANY INDEX   139

SUBJECT INDEX   141

Preface

This book grew out of my experience, over the last four years, teaching and then running Harvard Business School's required first-year course on Competition and Strategy. My colleagues and I were dissatisfied with the strategy textbooks and disinclined to assign a mish-mash of book chapters and articles instead. As a result, I, along with some of them, began to write conceptual notes for our students. These notes, which have since been revised several times, constitute the core of this book.

Strategy and the Business Landscape has several distinguishing features.

First and perhaps most obviously, it begins with and maintains a historical perspective on the field of strategy. This approach offers several advantages. It avoids imposing an arbitrary definition of strategy on the reader. Tracking changing conceptions of strategy can also help identify patterns in what might otherwise seem to be just the random churn of ideas. Most ambitiously, an understanding of the history of the field may foster an ability to sort through the continual barrage of new ideas—some good and others bad—about strategy.

Second, this book tries to be contemporary as well as historically grounded. Thus Chapter 2 begins by reviewing early work on environmental analysis, particularly Michael Porter's influential "five-forces" framework (which is standard practice), but goes on to discuss newer ways of thinking about the business landscape (which is not). Chapter 3 pursues a parallel line of development, starting with the early work on competitive positioning but culminating in the more recent conceptualizations of added value and rugged landscapes. Chapters 4 and 5 deal with dynamic issues—the sustainability of superior performance and the instrumental roles of capabilities and commitments—that most strategists have only begun to address since the mid-1980s.

Third, this book uses firm-centered, value-based logic to bridge some of the great debates about strategy. It addresses the debate about internal versus external focus by concentrating on the firm in relation to its environment, aided by the visual imagery of the business landscape. The debate about competition versus cooperation is channeled into the recognition that both kinds of relationships affect a firm's added value as well as its ability to sustain and appropriate some of that value over time. And the debate about the activity-system vs. resource-based views of the firm is dealt with at length in Chapter 5, which emphasizes both the complementarity of these two perspectives on strategy and the way in which they need to be extended.

Fourth, this book tries to be practical as well as rigorous. Key concepts are laid out succinctly (but with suggestions for additional reading in the notes).

They are illustrated with rich examples, often drawn from consulting work. In addition, the process of actually applying these concepts to real-world situations is discussed in some detail.

Finally, this book focuses on business- rather than corporate-level strategy. While strategies at the corporate and business levels intersect to some extent significant differences are also apparent in many of the management issues raised. In addition, corporate strategy may have less immediate relevance to most of the M.B.A. students taking an introductory course on strategy. Having said that, there are obviously a number of good readings on corporate strategy that can be assigned in conjunction with this book for a course whose scope extends to corporate- as well as business-level issues.

It would have been impossible to prepare this book without aid and support from a number of different quarters. My most obvious debt is to my coauthors on the individual chapters in this book, David J. Collis, Gary P. Pisano, and Jan W. Rivkin. Each pushed the chapter in which he was involved to a new level. Each also provided copious feedback on some of the other chapters in this book, although none of the three should be presumed to agree entirely with the end-product.

I am also greatly indebted to the other colleagues with whom I have taught the Competition and Strategy course at Harvard. All of them have stimulated and sharpened my thinking about business strategy, and some of them have commented on earlier drafts of the chapters in this book as well. I am especially grateful to Adam Brandenburger, for developing and helping educate me about a number of the key ideas in this book, as well as for reading and commenting on a number of the draft chapters.

I owe another very important debt to our students in the Competition and Strategy course, who were an invaluable source of feedback on earlier versions of the chapters in this book. Their perspective on what worked and what didn't greatly helped reorganize and refine the exposition in this book.

In addition, I should thank a number of reviewers for their guidance:

Ralph Biggadike, Columbia University
Tina Dacin, Texas A&M University
Daniel E. Levinthal, University of Pennsylvania
Joseph T. Mahoney, University of Illinois at Urbana-Champaign
George Puia, Indiana State University
John A. Seeger, Bentley College
Mark Shanley, Northwestern University
Todd Zenger, Washington University

Finally, I am also very grateful to the teams assembled by Addison Wesley Longman and Prentice Hall for their support of this project; to my research associates, Bret Baird and Courtenay Sprague, for helping me push this work toward completion; to my exceptionally able assistant, Sharilyn Steketee, who made the process as painless as possible; and to my wife, Anuradha Mitra Ghemawat. Thank you all.

Boston
May 2000

The Origins of Strategy

If we wish to increase the yield of grain in a certain field and on analysis it appears that the soil lacks potash, potash may be said to be the strategic (or limiting) factor.

—Chester I. Barnard

The term "strategy" . . . is intended to focus on the interdependence of the adversaries' decisions and on their expectations about each other's behavior.

—Thomas C. Schelling

Strategy can be defined as the determination of the basic long-term goals and objectives of an enterprise, and the adoption of courses of action and the allocation of resources necessary for carrying out those goals.

—Alfred D. Chandler, Jr.

This chapter reviews the history of strategic thinking about business through the mid-1970s. The historical perspective, which is maintained throughout this book, is attractive for at least three reasons:

- Despite thoughtful attempts over the decades to define "strategy" (see the quotes at the beginning of this chapter), a rash of manifestos continue to emerge that purport to redefine the term.[1] It would therefore be idiosyncratic to begin by tossing another definition onto that pile. Examining the history of strategic ideas and practice constitutes a less arbitrary approach to the study of strategy.

- The historical perspective organizes changing conceptions of strategy as envisioned or enacted by the participants in this field—academics, managers, and consultants—allowing us to identify patterns in what might otherwise seem to be the chaotic churn of ideas. Patterns of this sort are evident in all the chapters of this book: coevolution with the environment, the development and diffusion of particular strategic paradigms, paradigm shifts, the recycling of earlier ideas, and so on.

- Most ambitiously, the idea of path-dependence (one of the rallying cries of academic strategists since the mid-1980s) suggests that an understanding of the history of ideas about strategy is essential for having a more informed sense of where they might go in the future. This point is developed further in the last chapter of this book.

In this chapter, we briefly discuss the origins of strategic ideas. We begin with some background, including military antecedents and then move on to discuss ideas about strategy that were developed and disseminated by academics and consultants in the 1960s and early 1970s. We conclude by reviewing the dissatisfaction with the state of the field that had developed by the second half of the 1970s. In particular, the underdevelopment of two basic components of popular techniques for portfolio planning—environmental attractiveness and competitive positioning—set the stage for much of the subsequent work on these topics that is discussed in Chapters 2 and 3, respectively. Chapters 4 and 5 address the other weakness of portfolio planning by emphasizing the dynamic dimension of strategic thinking.

BACKGROUND

"Strategy" is a term that can be traced back to the ancient Greeks, who used it to mean a chief magistrate or a military commander-in-chief. Over the next two millennia, refinements of the concept of strategy continued to focus on military interpretations. Carl von Clausewitz's attempted synthesis in the first half of the nineteenth century is a particularly notable example: He wrote that whereas "tactics . . . [involve] the use of armed forces in the engagement, strategy [is] the use of engagements for the object of the war."[2] The adaptation of strategic terminology to a business context, however, had to await the Second Industrial Revolution, which began in the second half of the nineteenth century but really took off only in the twentieth century.[3]

The First Industrial Revolution (which spanned the mid-1700s to the mid-1800s) had failed to induce much in the way of strategic thinking or behavior. This failure can be chalked up to the inference that, while this period was marked by intense competition among industrial firms, virtually all of those companies lacked the power to influence market outcomes to any significant extent. Because the First Industrial Revolution was largely driven by the development of international trade in a few commodities (especially cotton), most businesses tended to remain small and to employ as little fixed capital as possible. The chaotic markets of this era led economists such as Adam Smith to describe market forces as an "invisible hand" that remained largely beyond the control of individual firms. Like the "butchers, bakers, and candlestick makers" of the medieval guild system, the small industrial and merchant firms of the time required little or no strategy in any of the senses described in the quotes at the beginning of this chapter.

The Second Industrial Revolution, which began in the last half of the nineteenth century in the United States, saw the emergence of strategy as a way to shape market forces and affect the competitive environment. In the United States, the construction of key railroads after 1850 made it possible to build mass markets for the first time. Along with improved access to capital and credit, mass markets encouraged large-scale investment to exploit economies of scale in production and economies of scope in distribution. In some capital-intensive industries, Adam Smith's "invisible hand" came to be supplemented by what Alfred D. Chandler, Jr., a famous historian, has termed the "visible hand" of professional managers. By the late nineteenth century, a new type of firm began to emerge, first in the United States and then in Europe: the large, vertically integrated company that invested heavily in manufacturing and marketing, and in management hierarchies to coordinate those functions. Over time, the largest companies of this sort began to alter the competitive environment within their industries and even cross industry boundaries.[4]

The need for explicitly strategic thinking was first articulated by high-level managers at these large companies. For example, Alfred Sloan, the chief executive of General Motors from 1923 to 1946, devised a successful strategy based on the perceived strengths and weaknesses of his company's critical competitor, the Ford Motor Company, and wrote it up after he retired.[5] In the 1930s, Chester Barnard, a senior executive with New Jersey Bell, argued that managers should pay especially close attention to "strategic factors" which depend on "personal or organizational action."[6]

World War II supplied a vital stimulus to strategic thinking in business as well as military domains, because it sharpened the problem of allocating scarce resources across the entire economy. New operations research techniques (for example, linear programming) were devised, which paved the way for the use of quantitative analysis in formal strategic planning. In 1944, John von Neumann and Oskar Morgenstern published their classic work, *The Theory of Games and Economic Behavior,* which solved the problem of zero-sum games (mostly military ones, from an aggregate perspective) and framed the issues surrounding non-zero-sum games (mostly business situations, which are discussed further in these terms in Chapter 4). Also, the concept of "learning curves" became an increasingly important tool for planning. The learning curve was first discovered in the military aircraft industry in the 1920s and 1930s, where manufacturers noticed that direct labor costs tended to decrease by a constant percentage as the cumulative quantity of aircraft produced doubled. Such learning effects figured prominently in wartime production planning efforts.

Wartime experiences encouraged not only the development of new tools and techniques, but also, in the view of some observers, the use of formal strategic thinking to guide management decisions. Peter Drucker, writing about this period, argued that "management is not just passive, adaptive behavior; it means taking action to make the desired results come to pass." He noted that economic theory had long treated markets as impersonal forces, beyond the control of individual entrepreneurs and organizations. In the age of large corporations, however, managing "implies responsibility for attempting to shape the economic environment, for planning, initiating and carrying through changes in that economic environment, for constantly pushing back the limitations of economic circumstances on the enterprise's freedom of action."[7] This insight became the key rationale for business strategy—that is, by consciously using formal planning, a company could exert some positive control over market forces.

These insights into the nature of strategy seemed, however, to lie fallow through the 1950s. In the United States, rationing or outright bans on production during World War II combined with high levels of private savings to create excess demand for many products. The Korean War provided a further boost in demand. Europe and Japan experienced even more severe postwar dislocations, which induced greater governmental control of what Lenin had called the "commanding heights" of an economy: its key industries and enterprises. Similar increases in governmental control, as opposed to reliance on market forces, were observed in poorer countries, including many of the new ones that emerged as colonialism unwound itself.[8]

A more direct bridge to the development of strategic concepts for business applications was provided by interservice competition in the U.S. military after World War II. During this period, American military leaders began debating which arrangements would best protect legitimate competition among military services while still maintaining the needed integration of strategic and tactical planning. Many argued that the Army, Navy, Marines, and Air Force would be more efficient if they were unified into a single organization. As the debate raged, Philip Selznick, a sociologist, noted that the Navy Department "emerged as the defender of subtle institutional values and tried many times to formulate the distinctive characteristics of the various services." In essence, "Navy spokesmen attempted to distinguish between the Army as a 'manpower' organization and the Navy as a finely adjusted system of technical, engineering skills—a 'machine-centered' organization. Faced with what it perceived as a mortal threat, the Navy became highly self-conscious about its distinctive competence."[9] The concept of "distinctive competence" had great resonance for strategic management, as we will see.

ACADEMIC UNDERPINNINGS

Eminent economists produced some of the earliest academic writings about strategy. For example, John Commons, an institutionalist, wrote in his 1934 book about business firms' focus on *strategic* or limiting factors in a way that was picked up a few years later—potash example and all—by Chester Barnard (see the first quote in the beginning of this chapter).[10] Ronald Coase, who might be called the first organizational economist, published a provocative article in 1937 that asked why firms exist—an article that continues to be cited six decades later, and garnered its author a Nobel Prize.[11] Joseph Schumpeter, a technologist, discussed in his 1942 book the idea that business strategy encompassed much more than the price-setting contemplated in orthodox microeconomics.[12] And a book published in 1959 by Edith Penrose explicitly related the growth of business firms to the resources under their control and the administrative framework used to coordinate their use.[13] Overall, however, economists had much less direct impact on the early evolution of academic thinking about business strategy than did academics located in business schools.

The Second Industrial Revolution witnessed the founding of many elite business schools in the United States, beginning with the Wharton School in 1881. The Harvard Business School, founded in 1908, was among the first to promote the idea that managers should be trained to think strategically rather than just acting as functional administrators, although strategy itself wasn't explicitly invoked until the 1960s. In 1912, Harvard introduced a required second-year course in "Business Policy," which was designed to integrate the knowledge gained in functional areas like accounting, operations, and finance. The goal was to give students a broader perspective on the strategic problems faced by corporate executives. A course description from 1917 claimed that "an analysis of any business problem shows not only its relation to other problems in the same group, but also the intimate connection of groups. Few problems in business are purely intradepartmental." Also, the policies of each department must maintain a "balance in accord with the underlying policies of the business as a whole."[14]

In the early 1950s, two professors of Business Policy at Harvard, George Albert Smith, Jr., and C. Roland Christensen, encouraged students to question whether a firm's strategy matched its competitive environment. In reading cases, students were taught to ask the following question: Do a company's policies "fit together into a program that effectively meets the requirements of the competitive situation?"[15] Students were told to address this problem by asking, "How is the whole industry doing? Is it growing and expanding? Is it static? Is it declining?" Then, having "sized up" the competitive environment, the student was to ask still more questions: "On what basis must any one company compete with the others in this particular industry? At what kinds of things does it have to be especially competent, in order to compete?"[16]

In the late 1950s, another Harvard Business Policy professor, Kenneth Andrews, expanded upon this thinking by arguing that "every business organization, every subunit of organization, and even every individual [ought to] have a clearly defined set of purposes or goals which keeps it moving in a *deliberately chosen direction* and prevents its drifting in undesired directions" (emphasis added). Like Alfred Sloan at General Motors, Andrews thought that "the primary function of the general manager, over time, is supervision of the continuous process of determining the nature of the enterprise and setting, revising and attempting to achieve its goals."[17] His conclusions were motivated by an industry note and company cases that Andrews prepared on Swiss watchmakers, which uncovered significant differences in performance associated with different strategies for competing in that industry.[18] This format of combining industry notes with company cases soon became the norm in Harvard's Business Policy course.[19]

In the 1960s, classroom discussions in business schools came to focus on matching a company's "strengths" and "weaknesses"—its distinctive competence—with the "opportunities" and "threats" (or risks) that it faced in the

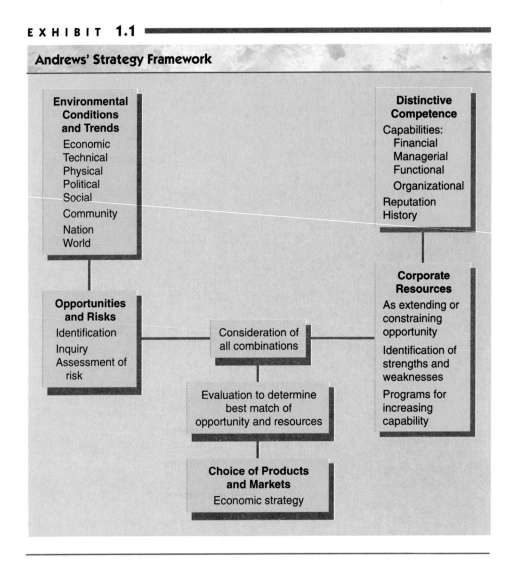

Andrews' Strategy Framework

marketplace. This framework, which came to be referred to by the acronym SWOT, represented a major step forward in bringing explicitly competitive thinking to bear on questions of strategy. Kenneth Andrews combined these elements in a way that emphasized that competencies or resources had to match environmental needs to have value (see Exhibit 1.1).[20]

In 1963, a business policy conference was held at Harvard that helped diffuse the SWOT concept in both academia and management practice. Attendance at the conference was heavy, but the ensuing popularity of SWOT—which was still used by many firms in the 1990s, including Wal*Mart—did not bring closure to the problem of actually defining a firm's distinctive competence. To solve this problem, strategists had to decide which aspects of the firm were "enduring and unchanging over relatively long periods of time" and which were "necessarily more responsive to changes in the marketplace and the pressures of other environmental forces." This distinction was crucial because "the *strategic* decision is concerned with the long-term development of the enterprise" (emphasis added).[21] When strategy choices were analyzed from a long-range perspective, the idea of "distinctive competence" took on added importance because most long-run investments involved greater risks. Thus, if the opportunities a firm was pursuing appeared "to outrun [its] present distinctive competence," then the strategist had to consider a firm's "willingness to gamble that the latter can be built up to the required level."[22]

The debate over a firm's "willingness to gamble" on its distinctive competence in its pursuit of an opportunity continued throughout the 1960s, fueled by a booming stock market and corporate strategies that were heavily geared toward growth and diversification. In a classic 1960 article that anticipated this debate, titled "Marketing Myopia," Theodore Levitt had been sharply critical of any firm that focused too narrowly on delivering a specific product, presumably exploiting its distinctive competence, rather than consciously serving the customer. Levitt argued that when companies fail, "it usually means that the product fails to adapt to the constantly changing patterns of consumer needs and tastes, to new and modified marketing institutions and practices, or to product developments in complementary industries."[23]

Another leading strategist, Igor Ansoff, disagreed with this position, arguing that Levitt asked companies to take unnecessary risks by investing in new products that might not match the firm's distinctive competence. Ansoff suggested that a company should first ask whether a new product had a "common thread" with its existing products. He defined the common thread as a firm's "mission" or its commitment to exploit an existing need in the market as a whole.[24] According to Ansoff, "sometimes the customer is erroneously identified as the common thread of a firm's business. In reality a given type of customer will frequently have a range of unrelated product missions or needs."[25] To enable a firm to maintain its strategic focus, Ansoff suggested four categories for defining the common thread in its business/corporate strategy, as depicted in Exhibit 1.2.[26] Ansoff and others also worked to translate the logic built into the SWOT framework into complex flowcharts of concrete questions that needed to be answered in the development of strategies.[27]

In the 1960s, diversification and technological changes increased the complexity of the strategic situations that many companies faced, and their need for more sophisticated measures that could be used to evaluate and compare many different types of businesses. Because academics at business schools remained strongly wedded to the idea that strategies could be analyzed only on a case-by-case basis that accounted for the unique characteristics of every business, corporations turned elsewhere to satisfy their craving for standardized approaches to strategy

E X H I B I T **1.2**

Ansoff's Product/Mission Matrix

	Present Product	New Product
Present Mission	Market penetration	Product development
New Mission	Market development	Diversification

making.[28] According to a study conducted by the Stanford Research Institute, most large U.S. companies had set up formal planning departments by 1963.[29] Some of these internal efforts were quite elaborate.

General Electric (GE) served as a bellwether in developing its planning: It used business school faculty quite extensively in its executive education programs, but also developed an elaborate computer-based "Profitability Optimization Model" (PROM) on its own in the early 1960s that appeared to explain a significant fraction of the variation in the return on investment afforded by its various businesses.[30] Over time, like many other companies, GE also sought the help of private consulting firms. Although consultants made multifaceted contributions to business (for example, to planning, forecasting, logistics, and long-range research and development), the next section focuses on their impact on mainstream strategic thinking.

THE RISE OF STRATEGY CONSULTANTS

The 1960s and early 1970s witnessed the rise of a number of strategy consulting practices. In particular, the Boston Consulting Group (BCG), founded in 1963, had a major impact on the field by applying quantitative research to problems of business and corporate strategy. BCG's founder, Bruce Henderson, believed that a consultant's job was to find "meaningful quantitative relationships" between a company and its chosen markets.[31] In his words, "good strategy must be based primarily on logic, not . . . on experience derived from intuition."[32] Indeed, Henderson was utterly convinced that economic theory would eventually lead to the development of a set of universal rules for strategy. As he explained, "in most firms strategy tends to be intuitive and based upon traditional patterns of behavior which have been successful in the past." In contrast, "in growth industries or in a changing environment, this kind of strategy is rarely adequate. The accelerating rate of change is producing a business world in which customary managerial habits and organization are increasingly inadequate." [33]

To help executives make effective strategic decisions, BCG drew on the existing knowledge base in academia: One of its first employees, Seymour Tilles, was formerly a lecturer in Harvard's Business Policy course. BCG also struck off in a new direction that Bruce Henderson described as "the business of selling powerful oversimplifications." [34] In fact, BCG came to be known as a "strategy boutique"—early in its history, its business was largely based on a single concept: the experience curve (discussed below). Using a single concept proved valuable because "in nearly all problem solving there is a universe of alternative choices, most of which must be discarded without more than cursory attention." Hence, some "frame of reference is needed to screen the . . . relevance of data, methodology, and implicit value judgments" involved in any strategy decision. Given that decision making is necessarily a complex process, the most useful "frame of reference is the concept. Conceptual thinking is the skeleton or the framework on which all other choices are sorted out." [35]

BCG and the Experience Curve

BCG first developed its version of the learning curve—what it labeled the "experience curve"—in 1965–1966. According to Bruce Henderson, "it was developed to try to explain price and competitive behavior in the extremely fast growing segments" of industries for clients such as Texas Instruments and Black and Decker. [36] As BCG consultants studied these industries, they naturally asked, "[why does] one competitor [outperform] another (assuming comparable management skills and resources)? Are there basic rules for success? There, indeed, appear to be rules for success, and they relate to the impact of accumulated experience on competitors' costs, industry prices and the interrelation between the two." [37]

The firm's standard claim for the experience curve was that, for each cumulative doubling of experience, *total* costs would decline roughly 20% to 30% because of economies of scale, organizational learning and technological innovation. Exhibit 1.3 illustrates one example of the experience effect. According to BCG's explanation of its strategic implications, "the producer . . . who has made the most units should have the lowest costs and the highest profits." [38] Bruce Henderson claimed that with the experience curve, "the stability of competitive relationships should be predictable, the value of market share change should be calculable, [and] the effects of growth rate should [also] be calculable." [39]

From the Experience Curve to Portfolio Analysis

By the early 1970s, the experience curve had led to another "powerful oversimplification" by BCG: the so-called growth-share matrix, which represented the first use of portfolio analysis. With this matrix, after experience curves were drawn for

E X H I B I T 1.3

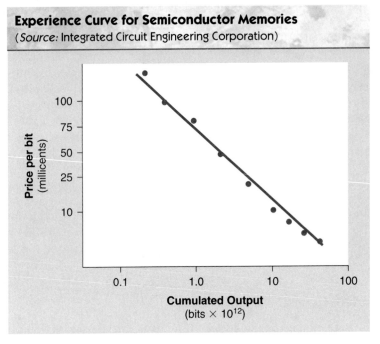

Experience Curve for Semiconductor Memories
(*Source:* Integrated Circuit Engineering Corporation)

each of a diversified company's business units, the business units' relative potential as areas for investment could be compared by plotting them on the grid shown in Exhibit 1.4.[40]

BCG's basic strategy recommendation was to maintain a balance between "cash cows" (that is, mature businesses) and "stars," while allocating some resources to feed "question marks" (that is, potential stars). "Dogs" were to be sold off. Using more sophisticated language, a BCG vice president explained that "since the producer with the largest stable market share eventually has the lowest costs and greatest profits, it becomes vital to have a dominant market share in as many products as possible. However, market share in slowly growing products can be gained only by reducing the share of competitors who are likely to fight back." If a product market is growing rapidly, "a company can gain share by securing most of the *growth*. Thus, while competitors grow, the company can grow even faster and emerge with a dominant share when growth eventually slows."[41]

Strategic Business Units and Portfolio Analysis

Numerous other consulting firms developed their own matrices for portfolio analysis at roughly the same time as BCG. McKinsey & Company's effort, for instance, began in 1968 when Fred Borch, the CEO of GE, asked McKinsey to examine GE's corporate structure. At the time, GE consisted of 200 profit centers

EXHIBIT **1.4**

BCG's Growth-Share Matrix

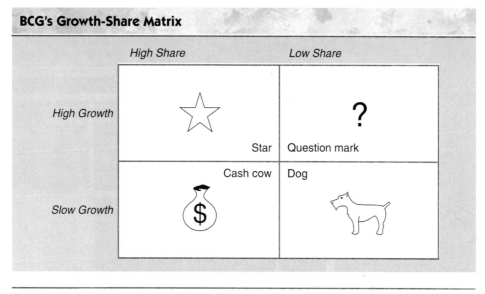

and 145 departments arranged around 10 groups. The boundaries for these units had been defined according to theories of financial control, which the McKinsey consultants judged to be inadequate. They argued instead that the firm should be organized on more strategic lines, with greater concern for external conditions than for internal controls, and a more future-oriented approach than was possible using measures of past financial performance. McKinsey's study recommended a formal strategic planning system, which would divide the company into "natural business units," which Borch later renamed "strategic business units" (or SBUs). GE's executives followed this advice, which took two years to implement.

In 1971, however, a GE corporate executive asked McKinsey to evaluate the strategic plans that were being written by the company's many SBUs. GE had already considered using the BCG growth-share matrix to decide the fate of its SBUs, but its top management had decided then that they could not set priorities on the basis of just two performance measures. After studying the problem for three months, a McKinsey team produced what came to be known as the GE/McKinsey nine-block matrix (see Exhibit 1.5).[42] The nine-block matrix used approximately one dozen measures to screen for industry attractiveness and another dozen to screen for competitive position, although the weights attached to those measures were not specified.[43]

Another, more quantitative approach to portfolio planning was developed at roughly the same time under the aegis of the "Profit Impact of Market Strategies" (PIMS) program. PIMS was the multicompany successor to the PROM program that GE had started a decade earlier. By the mid-1970s, PIMS contained data on 620 SBUs drawn from 57 diversified corporations.[44] These data were originally

The Industry Attractiveness–Business Strength Matrix

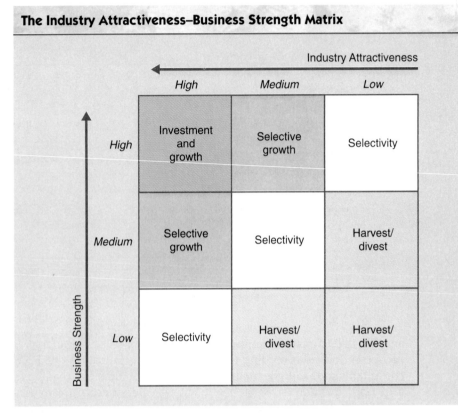

used to explore the determinants of returns on investment by regressing historical returns on several dozen variables, including market share, product quality, investment intensity, and marketing and R&D expenditures. The regressions established what were supposed to be benchmarks for the *potential* performance of SBUs with particular characteristics against which their *actual* performance might be compared.

In these applications, segmenting diversified corporations into SBUs became recognized as an important precursor to analyzing economic performance.[45] This step forced "deaveraging" of cost and performance numbers that had previously been calculated at more aggregated levels. In addition, it was thought that with such approaches, "strategic thinking was appropriately pushed 'down the line' to managers closer to the particular industry and its competitive conditions."[46]

In the 1970s, virtually every major consulting firm used some type of portfolio analysis—either a variant on the two matrices already discussed or its own internally developed program (for example, Arthur D. Little's 24-box life-cycle matrix)—to generate strategy recommendations. Portfolio analyses became especially popular after the oil crisis of 1973 forced many large corporations to rethink, if not discard, their existing long-range plans. A McKinsey consultant noted that with "the sudden quadrupling of energy costs [due to the OPEC embargo], followed by a recession and rumors of impending capital crisis, [the job of] setting long-term growth and diversification objectives was suddenly an exercise in irrelevance." Now, strategic planning meant "sorting out winners and losers, setting priorities, and husbanding capital." In a climate where "product and geographic markets were depressed and capital was presumed to be short," [47] portfolio analysis gave executives a ready excuse to get rid of underperforming business units while directing more funds to the "stars." By 1979, as a survey of the *Fortune* 500 industrial companies concluded, 45% of those firms had introduced some type of portfolio planning techniques.[48]

EMERGING PROBLEMS

Somewhat ironically, the very macroeconomic conditions that (initially) increased the popularity of portfolio analysis also inspired questions about the experience curve. The high inflation and excess capacity (due to downturns in demand) induced by the oil shocks of 1973 and 1979 disrupted historical experience curves in many industries, suggesting that Bruce Henderson had oversold the concept in a 1974 pamphlet entitled, "Why Costs Go Down Forever." Another problem with the experience curve was pinpointed by a classic 1974 article by William Abernathy and Kenneth Wayne, which argued that "the consequence of intensively pursuing a cost-minimization strategy [for example, one based on the experience curve] is a reduced ability to make innovative changes and to respond to those introduced by competitors." [49] Abernathy and Wayne pointed to the case of Henry Ford, whose obsession with lowering costs had left him vulnerable to Alfred Sloan's strategy of product innovation in the car business. The concept of the experience curve also drew criticism for treating cost reductions as automatic rather than something to be managed, for assuming that most experience could be kept proprietary instead of spilling over to competitors, for mixing up different sources of cost reduction with very different strategic implications (for example, learning versus scale versus exogenous technical progress), and for leading to stalemates as more than one competitor pursued the same generic success factor.[50]

In the late 1970s, portfolio analysis came under attack as well. One problem was that the strategic recommendations for an SBU were often inordinately sensitive to the specific portfolio-analytic technique employed. For instance, when an academic study applied four different portfolio techniques to a group of 15 SBUs owned by the same *Fortune* 500 corporation, it found that only one out of the 15 SBUs fell in the same area of each of the four matrices and only five of the SBUs were classified similarly in three of the four matrices.[51] This level of concordance was only slightly higher than would have been expected if the 15 SBUs had been randomly classified four separate times!

Portfolio analysis was also associated with an even more serious set of difficulties: Even if one could figure out the "right" technique to employ, the mechanical determination of resource allocation patterns on the basis of historical performance data was inherently problematic, as was the implicit assumption that financial capital was *the* scarce resource on which top management had to focus. Some consultants readily acknowledged these problems. In 1979, Fred Gluck, the head of McKinsey's strategic management practice, ventured the opinion that "the heavy dependence on 'packaged' techniques [has] frequently resulted in nothing more than a tightening up, or fine tuning, of current initiatives within the traditionally configured businesses." Even worse, technique-based strategies "rarely beat existing competition" and often leave businesses "vulnerable to unexpected thrusts from companies not previously considered competitors."[52] Gluck and his colleagues sought to loosen some of the constraints imposed by mechanistic approaches by proposing that successful companies' strategies progress through four phases (depicted in Exhibit 1.6) that involve grappling with increasing levels of dynamism, multidimensionality, and uncertainty, and that therefore become less amenable to routine quantitative analysis.[53]

The most stinging attack on the analytical techniques popularized by strategy consultants was offered by two Harvard professors of production, Robert Hayes and William Abernathy, in 1980. They argued that "these new principles [of management], despite their sophistication and widespread usefulness, encourage a preference for (1) analytic detachment rather than the insight that comes from 'hands on experience' and (2) short-term cost reduction rather than long-term development of technological competitiveness."[54] Hayes and Abernathy criticized portfolio analysis especially as a tool that led managers to focus on minimiz-

E X H I B I T 1.6

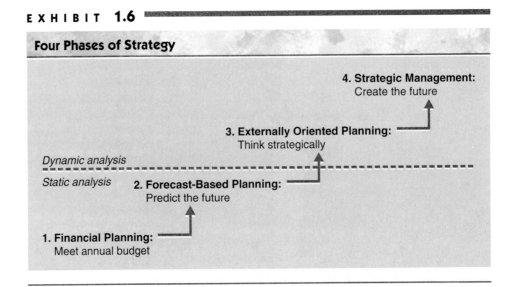

Four Phases of Strategy

4. **Strategic Management:**
Create the future

3. **Externally Oriented Planning:**
Think strategically

Dynamic analysis
- -
Static analysis   2. **Forecast-Based Planning:**
Predict the future

1. **Financial Planning:**
Meet annual budget

E X H I B I T 1.7

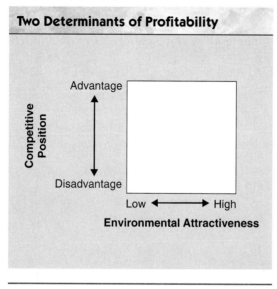

Two Determinants of Profitability

ing financial risks rather than investing in new opportunities that required a long-term commitment of resources.[55] They went on to compare U.S. firms unfavorably with Japanese and, especially, European companies.

These and other criticisms gradually diminished the popularity of portfolio analysis. Its rise and fall did have a lasting influence on subsequent work on competition and business strategy, however, because it drew attention to the need for more careful analysis of the two basic dimensions of portfolio-analytic grids shown in Exhibit 1.7: industry attractiveness and competitive position. Although these two dimensions had been identified earlier—in the General Survey Outline developed by McKinsey & Company for its internal use in 1952, for example— portfolio analysis underscored this particular way of analyzing the effects of competition on business performance. U.S. managers, in particular, proved avid consumers of additional insights about competition, partly because the exposure of much of U.S. industry to competitive forces increased dramatically during the 1960s and 1970s. Indeed, one economist estimated that the share of the U.S. economy that was subject to effective competition rose from 56% in 1958 to 77% by 1980 due to heightened import competition, antitrust actions, and deregulation.[56]

SUMMARY

This chapter reviewed the history of strategic thinking about business through the mid-1970s. The early history of business-strategic thinking was affected in many ways by military concepts and considerations. Sociology seems to have been the academic field that, with its construct of distinctive competence, wielded the most influence on the early elaborations of the concept of strategy in business, mostly by professors at business schools.[57] Consulting firms helped disseminate academic insights and developed a set of tools to help top managers (even of very highly diversified companies) monitor the strategies of the business units under them. Although disillusionment with specific tools quickly emerged, this line of work nevertheless framed the agenda for future research and development in the field of strategy.

GLOSSARY

distinctive competence
experience curve
learning curves
portfolio analysis

strategic business units or SBUs
strategy
SWOT

NOTES

1. Consult, for instance, the two McKinsey Award winners from the 1996 volume of the *Harvard Business Review:* "Strategy as Revolution" by Gary Hamel and "What Is Strategy?" by Michael Porter.
2. Carl von Clausewitz, *On War*. Edited and translated by Michael Howard and Peter Paret. (Princeton, NJ: Princeton University Press, 1984, © 1976), p. 128.
3. For a depiction of business history in terms of these industrial revolutions and a third one, see Thomas K. McCraw, ed., *Creating Modern Capitalism: How Entrepreneurs, Companies, and Countries Triumphed in Three Industrial Revolutions* (Cambridge, MA: Harvard University Press, 1998).
4. Alfred D. Chandler, Jr., *Strategy and Structure* (Cambridge, MA: MIT Press, 1963) and *Scale and Scope* (Cambridge, MA: Harvard University Press, 1990).
5. See Alfred P. Sloan, Jr., *My Years with General Motors* (New York: Doubleday, 1963).
6. Chester I. Barnard, *The Functions of the Executive* (Cambridge, MA: Harvard University Press, 1968; first published 1938), pp. 204–205.
7. Peter Drucker, *The Practice of Management* (New York: Harper & Row, 1954), p. 11.
8. Daniel Yergin and Joseph Stanislaw, *The Commanding Heights: The Battle Between Government and the Marketplace That Is Remaking the Modern World* (New York: Simon & Schuster, 1998).
9. Philip Selznick, *Leadership in Administration* (Evanston, IL: Row, Peterson, 1957), pp. 49–50.
10. John R. Commons, *Institutional Economics* (New York: MacMillan, 1934) and Chester I. Barnard, *The Functions of the Executive* (Cambridge, MA: Harvard University Press, 1938).
11. Ronald H. Coase, "The Nature of the Firm," *Economica N.S.*, 1937; 4:386–405. Reprinted In G. J. Stigler and K. E. Bouldings, eds., *Readings in Price Theory* (Homewood, IL: Richard D. Irwin, 1952). In addition to Coase's article, which influenced thinking about both strategy and organizations, a number of other authors made pioneering contributions to organizational theory that cannot be fully recognized here: Henri Fayol on administrative theory, Elton Mayo and Melville Dalton on human relations, and Herbert Simon and James March on information processing, to cite just a few.
12. Joseph A. Schumpeter *Capitalism, Socialism, and Democracy* (New York: Harper, 1942).
13. Edith T. Penrose, *The Theory of the Growth of the Firm* (Oxford: Basil Blackwell, 1959).
14. Official Register of Harvard University, March 29, 1917, pp. 42–43.
15. George Albert Smith, Jr., and C. Roland Christensen, *Suggestions to Instructors on Policy Formulation* (Homewood, IL: Richard D. Irwin, 1951), pp. 3–4.
16. George Albert Smith, Jr., *Policy Formulation and Administration* (Homewood, IL: Richard D. Irwin, 1951), p. 14.
17. Kenneth R. Andrews, *The Concept of Corporate Strategy* (Homewood, IL: Dow Jones-Irwin, 1971), p. 23.
18. See Part I of Edmund P. Learned, C. Roland Christensen, and Kenneth R. Andrews, *Problems of General Management* (Homewood, IL: Richard D. Irwin, 1961).

19. Interview with Kenneth Andrews, April 2, 1997.
20. Kenneth R. Andrews, *The Concept of Corporate Strategy*, revised ed. (Homewood, IL: Richard D. Irwin, 1980), p. 69.
21. Kenneth R. Andrews, *The Concept of Corporate Strategy* (Homewood, IL: Dow Jones-Irwin, 1971), p. 29.
22. Kenneth R. Andrews, op. cit., p. 100.
23. Theodore Levitt, "Marketing Myopia," *Harvard Business Review* July–August 1960:45–56.
24. Igor Ansoff, *Corporate Strategy* (New York: McGraw-Hill, 1965), pp. 106–109.
25. Igor Ansoff, op. cit., pp. 105–108.
26. Exhibit 1.2 is based on Henry Mintzberg's adaptation of Ansoff's matrix. Henry Mintzberg, "Generic Strategies," in *Advances in Strategic Management*, vol. 5 (Greenwich, CT: JAI Press, 1988), p. 2. For the original, see Igor Ansoff, *Corporate Strategy* (New York: McGraw-Hill, 1965), p. 128.
27. Michael E. Porter, "Industrial Organization and the Evolution of Concepts for Strategic Planning," in T. H. Naylor, ed., *Corporate Strategy* (New York: North-Holland, 1982), p. 184.
28. Adam M. Brandenburger, Michael E. Porter, and Nicolaj Siggelkow, "Competition and Strategy: The Emergence of a Field," paper presented at McArthur Symposium, Harvard Business School, October 9, 1996, pp. 3–4.
29. Stanford Research Institute, "Planning in Business, " Menlo Park, CA, 1963.
30. Sidney E. Schoeffler, Robert D. Buzzell, and Donald F. Heany, "Impact of Strategic Planning on Profit Performance," *Harvard Business Review* March–April 1974:137–145.
31. Interview with Seymour Tilles, October 24, 1996. Tilles credits Henderson for recognizing the competitiveness of Japanese industry at a time, in the late 1960s, when few Americans believed that Japan or any other country could compete successfully against American industry.
32. Bruce D. Henderson, *The Logic of Business Strategy* (Cambridge, MA: Ballinger Publishing, 1984), p. 10.
33. Bruce D. Henderson, *Henderson on Corporate Strategy* (Cambridge, MA: Abt Books, 1979), pp. 6–7.
34. Interview with Seymour Tilles, October 24, 1996.
35. Bruce D. Henderson, *Henderson on Corporate Strategy* (Cambridge, MA: Abt Books, 1979), p. 41.
36. Bruce Henderson explained that unlike earlier versions of the "learning curve," BCG's experience curve "encompasses all costs (including capital, administrative, research, and marketing) and traces them through technological displacement

and product evolution. It is also based on cash flow rates, not accounting allocation." Bruce D. Henderson, preface to Boston Consulting Group, *Perspectives on Experience* (Boston: BCG, 1972; first published 1968).
37. Boston Consulting Group, op. cit., p. 7.
38. Patrick Conley, "Experience Curves as a Planning Tool," BCG Pamphlet (1970), p. 15.
39. Bruce Henderson, preface, Boston Consulting Group, *Perspectives on Experience* (Boston: BCG, 1972; first published 1968).
40. See George Stalk, Jr., and Thomas M. Hout, *Competing Against Time* (New York: Free Press, 1990), p. 12.
41. Patrick Conley, "Experience Curves as a Planning Tool," BCG Pamphlet (197) pp. 10–11.
42. Arnoldo C. Hax and Nicolas S. Majluf, *Strategic Management: An Integrative Perspective* (Englewood Cliffs, NJ: Prentice-Hall, 1984), p. 156.
43. Interview with Mike Allen, April 4, 1997.
44. Sidney E. Schoeffler, Robert D. Buzzell, and Donald F. Heany, "Impact of Strategic Planning on Profit Performance," *Harvard Business Review* March–April 1974:137–145.
45. See Walter Kiechel, "Corporate Strategists Under Fire," *Fortune*, December 27, 1982.
46. Frederick W. Gluck and Stephen P. Kaufman, "Using the Strategic Planning Framework," McKinsey internal document in *Readings in Strategy* (1979), pp. 3–4.
47. J. Quincy Hunsicker, "Strategic Planning: A Chinese Dinner?," McKinsey staff paper (December 1978), p. 3.
48. Philippe Haspeslagh, "Portfolio Planning: Uses and Limits," *Harvard Business Review* January–February 1982:58–73.
49. William J. Abernathy and Kenneth Wayne, "Limits of the Learning Curve," *Harvard Business Review* September–October 1974:109–119.
50. Pankaj Ghemawat, "Building Strategy on the Experience Curve," *Harvard Business Review* March–April 1985:143–149.
51. Yoram Wind, Vijay Mahajan, and Donald J. Swire, "An Empirical Comparison of Standardized Portfolio Models," *Journal of Marketing* 1983; 47:89–99. The statistical analysis of Wind et al.'s results is based on an unpublished draft by Pankaj Ghemawat.
52. Frederick W. Gluck and Stephen P. Kaufman, "Using the Strategic Planning Framework," McKinsey internal document in *Readings in Strategy* (1979), pp. 5–6.
53. Adapted from Frederick W. Gluck, Stephen P. Kaufman, and A. Steven Walleck, "The Evolution

of Strategic Management," McKinsey staff paper (October 1978), p. 4. Reproduced in modified form in the same authors' "Strategic Management for Competitive Advantage," *Harvard Business Review* July–August 1980:154–161.

54. Robert H. Hayes and William J. Abernathy, "Managing Our Way to Economic Decline," *Harvard Business Review* July–August 1980:67–77.

55. Robert H. Hayes and William J. Abernathy, *ibid.* p. 71.

56. William G. Shepherd, "Causes of Increased Competition in the U.S. Economy, 1939–1980," *Review of Economics and Statistics* November 1982:613–626.

57. The doctrine of distinctive competence has been recycled, with great success, in the 1990s. See the discussion in Chapter 5.

Mapping the Business Landscape

Pankaj Ghemawat and David Collis[1]

> When an industry with a reputation for difficult economics meets a manager with a reputation for excellence, it is usually the industry that keeps its reputation intact.
>
> —*Warren Buffet*

M r. Buffet may have overstated the case. Nevertheless, there *is* considerable evidence in support of the presumption—explicit in the portfolio planning techniques discussed in Chapter 1—that the industry environment in which a business operates has a strong influence on its economic performance. Business strategists have used sophisticated statistical methods to show that 10%–20% of the observed variation in businesses' profitability is accounted for by the lines of businesses in which they operate.[2] The key implication for managers—that the environment matters—is usually summarized in a chart depicting the extent to which average profitability differs across lines of business or industries or industry groups over long periods of time (see Exhibit 2.1 for an example).[3]

Exhibit 2.1 is a somewhat unusual example in that it subtracts the estimated costs of (equity) capital from reported profitability (return on equity) and simultaneously displays the size of each industry group in terms of the capital invested in it. This approach offers the advantage of linking accounting measures of profitability with economic measures of total value created or destroyed.

In addition, Exhibit 2.1 suggests a way of visualizing the profit potential afforded by the business environment—by mapping it into a *landscape* in which the vertical dimension captures the level of economic profitability (or unprofitability).[4] A two-dimensional landscape, such as the one shown in Exhibit 2.1, permits us to include just one dimension of choice (e.g., where to compete). A three-dimensional landscape, such as the one in Exhibit 2.2, allows for two dimensions of choice. Most businesses are best envisioned as operating in a high-dimension space of choices, with each location in this space representing a different *business model*—that is, a different set of choices about what to do and how to do it. A business landscape maps each business model's elevation according to its

E X H I B I T   2.1

Average Economic Profits of U.S. Industry Groups, 1978–1996 (*Sources:* Compustat, Value Line, and Marakon Associates Analysis)

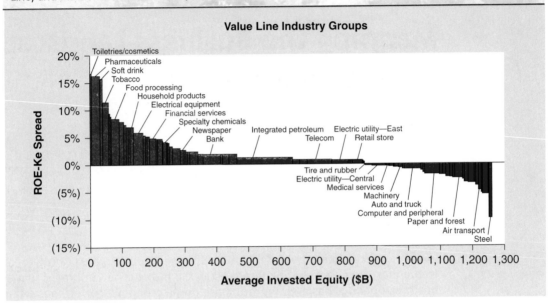

economic profitability. The central challenge of strategy is to guide a business to a relatively high point on this landscape.

In the chapters that follow, we will elaborate further on the landscape metaphor. In the context of this chapter, however, the business landscape helps us visualize the fact that the profitability of competitors in the same line of business or industry tends to have a common underlying component. Competitors are naturally grouped close together on the broader business landscape based on the business models they pursue. The common component of their profitability implies that the average height above (or below) sea level varies systematically across different parts of the business landscape. Reinterpreted in these terms, Exhibit 2.1 suggests that in the last quarter of the twentieth century, much of U.S. industry has operated, on average, close to sea level: More than half of all equity capital has been employed in industry groups with average returns on equity and costs of equity capital that fell within two percentage points of one another. It is also clear, however, that businesses in some industry groups (e.g., pharmaceuticals) have generally operated on high plateaus, whereas businesses in others (e.g., steel) have mostly remained stuck in deep troughs.

Managers' first-hand experience of such differences in average profitability across industries largely explains why many tend to take Warren Buffet seriously, despite his emphasis of the environmental constraints that limit what they can achieve. But managers need to do more than recognize how profitable particular arenas of competition have proved in the past. They also need to understand the

E X H I B I T 2.2

A Three-Dimensional Business Landscape

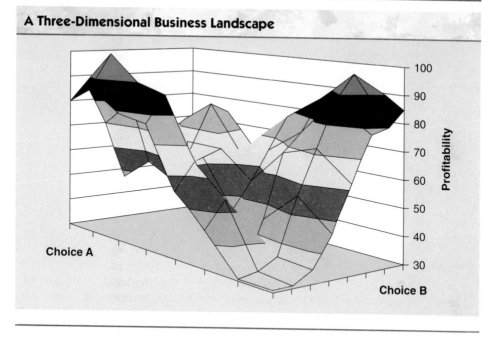

reasons behind such effects in order to decide where and how their firms will compete, to assess the implications of major changes in the relevant parts of the business landscape, and to adapt to or shape the business landscape.

Such ambitions combine with the complications inherent in the real world to place a sizable premium on finding simple, yet structured ways of thinking about business landscapes. This chapter begins by describing three successively more general structures that have been proposed as solutions to this problem: the supply-demand analysis of individual markets, the "five forces" framework for industry analysis developed by Michael Porter, and the "value net" devised more recently by Adam Brandenburger and Barry Nalebuff.[5] We then examine the actual process of mapping a business landscape in more detail.

The concept of the business landscape is deliberately meant to be broader than the usual conception of an "industry." Although this chapter focuses on so-called industry-level (or population-level) effects on performance, we want to explore such effects within a more complex, extensive set of relationships than the ones associated with traditional industry analysis.

SUPPLY-DEMAND ANALYSIS

Supply and demand are the grandparents of all attempts at landscape analysis. The idea that the interplay of supply and demand determines a natural price goes back—at least in Western culture—to the scholastic professors (mostly clerics) of

EXHIBIT 2.3

Supply-Demand Analysis

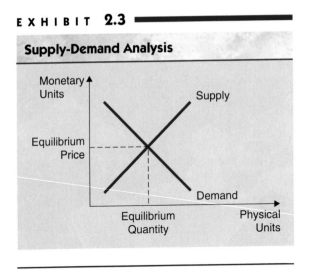

the Middle Ages.[6] Although many of the elements of supply-demand analysis were formalized by the scholastics and their successors, Alfred Marshall was the first (in the late nineteenth century) to combine them into the conventional supply-demand diagram depicted in Exhibit 2.3.

The development of the "Marshallian scissors" was motivated by the continuing debate about whether "value" was governed by supply-side costs or demand-side utility. This debate seemed no more reasonable to Marshall than disputes about whether the lower (or the upper) blade of a pair of scissors is the one that actually cuts paper. He suggested that price would instead be determined by the "equilibrium" point at which the demand curve for a particular product, summed across its buyers in decreasing order of their willingness to pay, intersected with its supply curve, summed across its suppliers in increasing order of their costs of production.[7]

The downward-sloping demand curve that underpins this line of analysis was treated as self-evident by Marshall, who also introduced the notion of the *price-elasticity of demand.* Demand is said to be relatively price-elastic if changes in price induce relatively large changes in the aggregate quantity demand (i.e., if the demand curve is close to horizontal); it is deemed relatively price-inelastic if the reverse is true (i.e., if the demand curve is close to vertical). On the supply side, Marshall argued that upward-sloping supply curves tend to become flatter—or even become horizontal—as the period lengthens. He got bogged down, however, when he attempted to analyze supply curves that slope downward rather than upward (i.e., display increasing returns to scale). Additionally, his analysis assumed that individual buyers and sellers would be small in relation to the size of the overall market and homogenous in the sense that a given buyer would have the same willingness to pay for the product of each supplier, and a given supplier would face the same costs in supplying its product to each buyer.

Supply-demand analysis was incorporated relatively quickly into economics and marketing courses at business schools. It seems to have had less impact on the teaching and practice of business strategy until the recessions of the 1970s and early 1980s, when downward shifts in demand curves reinforced the importance of developing a more thorough understanding of supply curves or, more accurately, cost curves that could help determine where prices settled down.

For an example of this sort of analysis, consider Exhibit 2.4, which traces the cost curve for hospitals in the Greater Boston area in 1991, as developed by Bain and Company, a consulting firm. This simple piece of analysis helped sensitize the high-cost Harvard Medical Center (HMC) teaching hospitals to the dire implications of the expected decrease in hospital utilization rates in Massachusetts from 80% in 1991 to 40%–60% by 1999, as "hospital bed days" per person declined from 1.2 per year toward the national average of 0.6 per year.[8]

This example also illustrates the limitations of Marshallian supply-demand analysis. First, it pushes the boundaries of reality to treat the hospitals in the local market as individually small and lacking market power. In fact, the two largest teaching hospitals affiliated with the HMC, Massachusetts General Hospital and Brigham and Women's Hospital, decided to join forces in the aftermath of Bain's study to attain a combined market share of 21% and improve their "clout." Second, it violates the assumption of homogeneity. Patients' needs differ, as do

E X H I B I T 2.4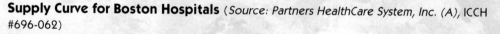

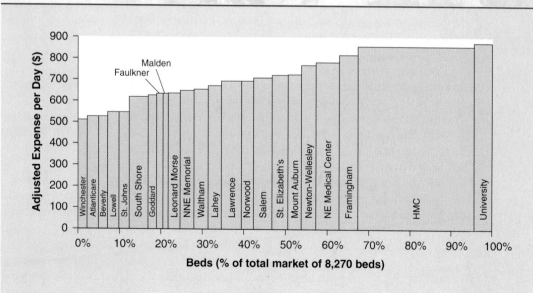

Supply Curve for Boston Hospitals (*Source: Partners HealthCare System, Inc. (A)*, ICCH #696-062)

hospitals' relative effectiveness in fulfilling those needs, to an extent that can only partially be controlled for by adjusting hospitals' costs on the basis of their case mix. It would therefore be useful to generalize the specializing assumptions made in supply-demand analysis, in this case and many others. The attempt to do so that has met with the greatest success among the business community is considered next, in its own historical context.

THE "FIVE FORCES" FRAMEWORK

The "large-numbers" assumption built into conventional supply-demand analysis had already been relaxed more than half a century before Marshall offered his synthesis. In 1838, Antoine Cournot provided the first analytical characterizations of equilibrium prices under monopoly and in the presence of duopolists (two sellers) independently deciding how much to produce.[9] The homogeneity assumption was relaxed in two books published in 1933, by Edward Chamberlin and Joan Robinson, in monopolistic competition—that is, situations in which the individual firm monopolized its own products but confronted a large number of competitors, similarly situated, that offered substitute products.[10] From a business-strategic perspective, however, these attempts to posit a large number of firms with different products that otherwise resembled one another offered few benefits: They missed the subtleties of *oligopolistic* competition (i.e., competition among the few).

A more important role was reserved for other economists in what came to be called the Harvard School, whose proponents argued that the *structure* of some industries might permit incumbent firms to earn positive economic profits over long periods of time.[11] Edward S. Mason, a member of the Harvard Economics Department, suggested that an industry's structure would determine the conduct of buyers and sellers—their choices of key decision variables—and, by implication, the industry's performance in terms of profitability, efficiency, and innovation.[12]

Joe Bain, also of the Harvard Economics Department (but unrelated to the consulting firm of the same name), sought to uncover relationships between industry structure and performance through empirical work focused on a limited number of structural variables. Two studies he published in the 1950s were particularly notable. The first study found that manufacturing industries in which the eight largest competitors accounted for more than 70% of sales were nearly twice as profitable as that of industries with eight-firm concentration ratios less than 70%.[13] The second study explained how, in certain industries, "established sellers can persistently raise their prices above a competitive level without attracting new firms to enter the industry."[14] Bain identified three basic barriers to entry: (1) an absolute cost advantage by an established firm (an enforceable patent, for instance); (2) a significant degree of product differentiation; and (3) economies of scale.

Bain's insights enabled the rapid growth of a new subfield of economics, known as industrial organization (IO), that explored the structural reasons why some industries were more profitable than others. By the mid-1970s, several hundred empirical studies in IO had been carried out. Although the relationships between structural variables and performance proved more complicated than earlier economists had suggested,[15] these studies did confirm that some industries are inherently much more profitable or "attractive," on average, than others.

IO's immediate impact on business strategy was limited by IO economists' focus on public, rather than private, policy and by the emphasis of Bain and his successors on using a short list of structural variables to explain industry profitability in a way that slighted business strategy. Both problems were addressed by Michael Porter, who had worked with another IO economist at Harvard, Richard Caves, to study industry structure and business strategy. In 1974, Porter prepared a "Note on the Structural Analysis of Industries" that represented his first attempt to turn IO on its head by focusing on the business policy objective of profit maximization, rather than the public policy objective of minimizing "excess" profits.[16] In 1980, he published his first book, *Competitive Strategy*, which owed much of its success to his "five forces" framework. This framework, which is reproduced in Exhibit 2.5, sought to relate the average profitability of the participants in an industry to five competitive forces.

Porter's framework for industry analysis generalized the supply-demand analysis of individual markets in several respects. First, it relaxed the assumptions of both large numbers and homogeneity—that is, of a large number of representative competitors. Second, along the vertical dimension, it shifted attention from two-stage vertical chains, each consisting of a supplier and buyer, to three-stage chains made up of suppliers, rivals, and buyers. Third, along the horizontal dimension, it accounted for potential entrants and substitutes as well as direct rivals. These generalizations, however, forced Porter to reach beyond scientific evidence into the realm of common sense. Indeed, a survey of empirical IO in the late 1980s—more than a decade after Porter first developed his framework—revealed that only a few of the influences that Porter flagged commanded strong empirical support.[17]

Despite such problems, the "five forces" framework's targeting of business concerns rather than public policy, its emphasis on extended competition for value rather than just competition among existing rivals, and its (relative) ease of application inspired numerous companies as well as business schools to adopt its use. A survey by Bain (the consulting firm) suggested a 25% usage rate in 1993.[18] Given the clear impact of Porter's "five forces" framework, we will discuss it in some detail. We will also illustrate the structural influences on industry profitability that the framework invokes by comparing two industry groups—steel and pharmaceuticals—located at the opposite ends of the business landscape depicted in Exhibit 2.1.

Force 1: The Degree of Rivalry

The intensity of rivalry is the most obvious of the five forces in an industry—and the one on which strategists have focused historically. It helps determine the extent to which the value created by an industry will be dissipated through head-

E X H I B I T   **2.5**

The "Five Forces" Framework for Industry Analysis (*Source:* Michael E. Porter, *Competitive Advantage* (New York: Free Press, 1985), p. 6)

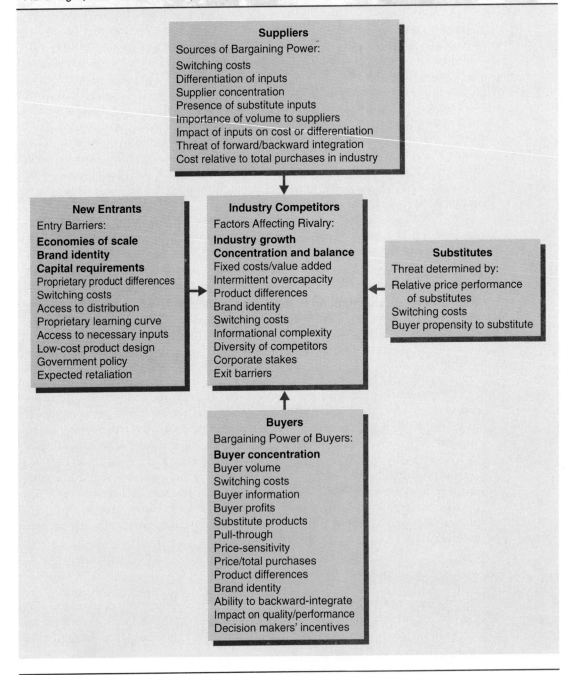

Suppliers

Sources of Bargaining Power:

Switching costs
Differentiation of inputs
Supplier concentration
Presence of substitute inputs
Importance of volume to suppliers
Impact of inputs on cost or differentiation
Threat of forward/backward integration
Cost relative to total purchases in industry

New Entrants

Entry Barriers:

Economies of scale
Brand identity
Capital requirements
Proprietary product differences
Switching costs
Access to distribution
Proprietary learning curve
Access to necessary inputs
Low-cost product design
Government policy
Expected retaliation

Industry Competitors

Factors Affecting Rivalry:

Industry growth
Concentration and balance
Fixed costs/value added
Intermittent overcapacity
Product differences
Brand identity
Switching costs
Informational complexity
Diversity of competitors
Corporate stakes
Exit barriers

Substitutes

Threat determined by:

Relative price performance
    of substitutes
Switching costs
Buyer propensity to substitute

Buyers

Bargaining Power of Buyers:

Buyer concentration
Buyer volume
Switching costs
Buyer information
Buyer profits
Substitute products
Pull-through
Price-sensitivity
Price/total purchases
Product differences
Brand identity
Ability to backward-integrate
Impact on quality/performance
Decision makers' incentives

to-head competition. The most valuable contribution of Porter's "five forces" framework, may be its suggestion that rivalry, while important, is only one of several forces that determine industry attractiveness.

The structural determinants of the degree of rivalry present in an industry are numerous. One set of conditions concerns the number and relative size of competitors. The more concentrated the industry, the more likely that competitors will recognize their mutual interdependence and so will restrain their rivalry. If, in contrast, the industry includes many small players, each will be apt to think that its effect on others will go unnoticed and so will be tempted to grab additional market share, thereby disrupting the market. For similar reasons, the presence of one dominant competitor rather than a set of equally balanced competitors may lessen rivalry: The dominant player may be able to set industry prices and discipline defectors, while equally sized players may try to outdo one another to gain an advantage.

A good example of these influences is seen in the U.S. steel industry, which was much more profitable before World War II than it has been in the postwar years. Competition in the prewar period was confined to a small number of domestic players led by U.S. Steel, which, as the dominant firm, represented an important source of stability. Some of U.S. Steel's attempts at stabilization weren't entirely legal, however. In the 1920s, for instance, its chairman, Judge Gary, became notorious for inviting competitors to dinner so that U.S. Steel could make its pricing policy clear to them. (This type of behavior also reduced "informational complexity," another item on Porter's list.) In the first few decades of the century, U.S. Steel, like a number of market leaders in other U.S. industries, helped prop up prices despite the erosion of its own market share over time.[19]

A second set of structural attributes that influence rivalry is more closely related to the industry's basic conditions. In capital-intensive industries, for example, the level of capacity utilization directly influences firms' incentive to engage in price competition to fill their plants. More generally, high fixed costs, excess capacity, slow growth, and lack of product differentiation all increase the degree of rivalry. In recent years, all of these attributes have been implicated as factors in the low profitability of the U.S. steel industry. In this industry, the ratio of fixed capital costs to value added is one of the highest in the U.S. economy, labor is largely a fixed cost, demand has been essentially flat, and minimal product differentiation has occurred, so that excess capacity has proved chronic and catastrophic in its effects.

The pharmaceutical industry presents a very different sort of picture. Fixed manufacturing costs are limited as a percentage of sales or value added. In fact, gross margins range as high as 90% for some blockbuster drugs. Demand has grown at double-digit rates, and differences among products, brand identity, and switching costs—discussed at greater length in the section "Force 4: Buyer Power"—have created insulation among competitors that is reinforced, in some cases, by patent protection.

Finally, the degree of rivalry also has behavioral determinants. If competitors are diverse, attach high strategic value to their positions in an industry, or face high exit barriers, they are more likely to compete aggressively. In steel, for instance, foreign competitors have, by adding diversity, helped shatter the domestic oligopolistic consensus. Strategic stakes have been high, because each domestic integrated steel maker has historically focused on steel as its core business. In addition, exit barriers have been compounded by the costs of cleaning up decommissioned sites.

Force 2: The Threat of Entry

Average industry profitability is influenced by both potential and existing competitors. The key concept in analyzing the threat of entry is entry barriers, which act to prevent an influx of firms into an industry whenever profits, adjusted for the cost of capital, rise above zero. In contrast, entry barriers exist whenever it is difficult or not economically feasible for an outsider to replicate the incumbents' positions. Entry barriers usually rest on irreversible resource commitments (discussed below).

Exhibit 2.5 illustrates the diverse forms that entry barriers can take. Some barriers reflect intrinsic physical or legal obstacles to entry. The most common forms of entry barriers, however, are usually the scale and the investment required to enter an industry as an efficient competitor. For example, when incumbent firms have well-established brand names and clearly differentiated products, a potential entrant may find it uneconomical to undertake the marketing campaign necessary to introduce its own products effectively. The magnitude of the required expenditures may be only part of the entrant's problem in such a situation: It may take years for the firm to build a reputation for product quality, no matter how large its initial advertising campaign is. Also, entry barriers are not given exogenously: They can be contrived along these dimensions and many others. Credible threats of retaliation by incumbents represent perhaps the clearest example.

To illustrate the difference that entry barriers can make, consider two very different *strategic groups*—as in two very different business models—within the pharmaceutical industry: research-based pharmaceutical companies versus manufacturers of generic pharmaceuticals. Research-based companies have been far more profitable on average, largely because they are protected by higher entry barriers. These barriers include patent protection, a new-drug development process that can cost hundreds of millions of dollars and stretch over more than a decade, carefully cultivated brand identities, and large sales forces that call on individual doctors. In contrast, the generic drug segment of the industry is characterized by a lack of patent protection, much smaller requirements of capital and time for product development, weak to nonexistent brand identities, and distribution efforts that focus on serving large accounts that purchase in bulk at low prices.

The steel industry illustrates that barriers to entry can, like other elements of industry structure, change over time. Integrated U.S. steel makers that manufactured steel from iron ore were long protected from competition by domestic entrants by the billion-plus dollars of capital required to build an efficiently scaled integrated steel mill (which ensured that no new integrated mills were built in the

United States for the last 40 years). Since the 1960s, however, integrated steel makers have come under intense pressure from minimills, which make steel from scrap rather than from iron ore. Minimill technology has essentially reduced the scale required for efficient operation by a factor of 10 (or more) and the investment required per ton of capacity by another factor of 10—leading, in some sense, to a hundredfold reduction in barriers to entry. As a result, profitability has collapsed in the segments of the steel industry that minimills have been able to penetrate.

Force 3: The Threat of Substitutes

The threat that substitutes pose to an industry's profitability depends on the relative price-to-performance ratios of the different types of products or services to which customers can turn to satisfy the same basic need. The threat of substitution is also affected by switching costs—that is, the costs in areas such as retraining, retooling, or redesign that are incurred when a customer switches to a different type of product or service. In many cases, the substitution process follows an S-shaped curve. It starts slowly as a few trendsetters risk experimenting with the substitute, picks up steam if other customers follow suit, and finally levels off when nearly all of the economical substitution possibilities have been exhausted.

Substitute materials that are putting pressure on the steel industry include plastics, aluminum, and ceramics. The industry also must reckon with the substitution threat associated with less-intensive use of steel in end-products such as cars. For a more specific example, consider the substitution of aluminum for steel in the metal can industry, which is described in some detail in the fourth case in this book, on Crown Cork & Seal. Aluminum's lighter weight and superior lithographic characteristics enable it to take volume away from steel despite higher prices. The costs to can makers of switching from steel to aluminum probably slowed substitution initially. In the 1980s, however, substitution sped up so that steel currently holds only a small share of the market, in niches such as food cans.

It is worth emphasizing that any analysis of the threat of (demand-side) substitution must look broadly at all products that perform similar functions for customers, not just at physically similar products. Thus substitutes for pharmaceuticals, broadly construed, might include preventive care and hospitalization. Indeed, there is probably some truth to the pharmaceutical industry's assertions that one major reason for its profitability and growth is the fact that pharmaceuticals represent a more cost-effective form of health care, in many cases, than hospitalization.

Conceptually, analysis of the substitution possibilities open to buyers should be supplemented by considering the possibilities available to suppliers.[20] Supply-side substitutability influences suppliers' willingness to provide required inputs, just as demand-side substitutability influences buyers' willingness to pay for products. Integrated steel makers that mix steel scrap with iron ore as inputs into their production processes, for example, have been unable to hold down scrap prices because of growing demand for scrap from minimills, which use it as their primary input.

Force 4: Buyer Power

Buyer power is one of the two vertical forces that influence the appropriation of the value created by an industry. It allows customers to squeeze industry margins by compelling competitors to either reduce prices or increase the level of service offered without recompense.

Probably the most important determinants of buyer power are the size and the concentration of customers. Such considerations help explain why auto makers, in particular, have historically enjoyed considerable leverage in dealing with steel makers. Other reasons include the extent to which they were well informed about steel makers' costs and the credibility of their threats to integrate backward into steel making (a strategy once adopted by Ford). In contrast, none of these sources of buyer power—concentration, good information, or the ability to backward-integrate—were evident, historically, in the pharmaceutical industry.

Buyer bargaining power can obviously be offset in situations in which competitors are themselves concentrated or differentiated. Both conditions have helped manufacturers of stainless and other specialty steels achieve higher rates of profitability than large, integrated steel makers. In the pharmaceutical industry, no substitutes are available for many patented drugs (e.g., Viagra): They must be purchased from a single manufacturer. Even when therapeutic substitutes are available, slight differences in their chemical composition can create large differences in their side-effects, yielding significant product differentiation.

It is often useful to distinguish potential buyer power from the buyer's willingness or incentive to use that power. For example, the U.S. government is potentially a very powerful purchaser of pharmaceuticals through its Medicaid and Medicare programs. Historically, however, it has refrained from exercising its potential power—a fortunate state of affairs for the pharmaceutical industry but an unfortunate one for taxpayers.

To explain why buyers do or do not have the incentive to use their inherent power, we must look at another, more behavioral set of conditions. One of the most important factors in this regard is the share of the purchasing industry's cost accounted for by the products in question. Purchasing decisions naturally focus on larger-cost items first. This fact of life has been a curse for the steel industry: Steel represents a major slice of the costs of many of the end-products in which it is used, from cans to cars.

Another important factor is the "risk of failure" associated with a product's use. In pharmaceuticals, patients often lack enough information to evaluate competing drugs and must take into account the high personal cost of any substitute's failure. This high personal cost of failure is also a consideration for doctors who prescribe drugs: The medical profession is quite concerned about malpractice suits. Generics tend to be seen as particularly risky, a perception that has not been alleviated by scandals involving some firms' substandard manufacturing practices. As a result, high-priced brands have been able to retain significant shares in many product categories even after satisfactory generic substitutes have reached the market.

The pharmaceutical industry example also highlights the importance of studying the decision-making process when analyzing buyer power. The interests and incentives of all players involved in the purchase decision must be understood if we are to predict the price-sensitivity of that decision. Many doctors and patients traditionally lacked incentives to hold down the prices paid for drugs because a third party—an insurance company—actually footed the bill. Today these incentives are changing, however, as the spread of managed care increases price-sensitivity.

Force 5: Supplier Power

Supplier power is the mirror image of buyer power. As a result, the analysis of supplier power typically focuses first on the relative size and concentration of suppliers relative to industry participants and second on the degree of differentiation in the inputs supplied. The ability to charge customers different prices in line with differences in the value created for each of those buyers usually indicates that the market is characterized by high supplier power (and low buyer power).

None of these considerations has been much of a problem for the pharmaceutical industry in the past. For conventional drugs (as opposed to biotechnological products), inputs are usually available from several commodity chemical companies. The U.S. integrated steel industry, in contrast, has been ravaged by the way in which supplier power has been wielded. The suppliers that have mattered the most have been the workers unionized by the United Steel Workers. Through collective action, these employees have historically been able to bargain their wages to levels well in excess of other manufacturing industries while protecting jobs. At the midpoint of the period considered in Exhibit 2.1, excess compensation and employment swallowed up as much as one-fourth of steel makers' total revenues!

We conclude this section by noting that relationships with buyers and suppliers have important cooperative as well as competitive elements. General Motors and other U.S. automobile companies lost sight of this fact when they pushed their parts suppliers to the wall by playing them against one another. Japanese car manufacturers, in contrast, committed themselves to long-run supplier relationships that paid off in terms of higher quality and faster new product development. The importance of both cooperation and competition is highlighted by the template for landscape analysis, the value net, that is discussed in the next section.

THE VALUE NET AND OTHER GENERALIZATIONS

The years since Porter first developed his "five forces" framework have seen the rearrangement and incorporation of additional variables (e.g., import competition and multimarket contact) into the determinants of the intensity of each of the five

E X H I B I T **2.6**

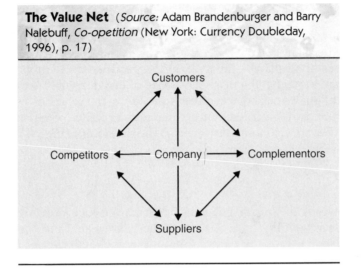

The Value Net (*Source:* Adam Brandenburger and Barry Nalebuff, *Co-opetition* (New York: Currency Doubleday, 1996), p. 17)

competitive forces. Even more important, the framework itself can be generalized substantially by bringing new types of players into the analysis. The most successful attempt to do so involves the value net framework devised by Adam Brandenburger and Barry Nalebuff (see Exhibit 2.6).[21]

The value net highlights the critical role that complementors—participants from which customers buy complementary products or services, or to which suppliers sell complementary resources—can play in influencing business success or failure. Complementors are defined as being the mirror image of competitors (including new entrants and substitutes as well as existing rivals). On the demand side, they increase buyers' willingness to pay for products; on the supply side, they decrease the price that suppliers require for their inputs.

To see why it is important to include complementors in the picture, reconsider the pharmaceutical industry example. Doctors greatly influence the success of these pharmaceutical manufacturers through their prescription of drugs, but they cannot, in most cases, be considered buyers: Money typically does not flow directly from them to the pharmaceutical manufacturers. Thus they are more naturally thought of as complementors who increase buyers' willingness to pay for particular products.

An even more powerful example is provided by computer hardware and software. Microsoft's Windows 95 operating system is far more valuable on a computer equipped with an Intel Pentium microprocessor than one containing a 486 chip, and vice versa. Yet Microsoft and Intel wouldn't show up on one another's "five forces" screens! Common sense nevertheless suggests that Intel should regard Microsoft as an important player in the business landscape on which it operates, and vice versa. The importance of this insight is reinforced by recent reports of wobbles in the "Wintel" axis, as divergences in the interests of these two players appear to be creating some problems for both of them. Intel has, in fact, begun to incorporate complementors into its environmental scans according to its chairman, Andy Grove.[22]

Complementors are a ubiquitous feature of many business landscapes.[23] They seem to be particularly important in situations where businesses are developing entirely new ways of doing things or where standards play important roles in combining very different kinds of expertise into systems that work well. In the early days of the automobile industry, for instance, General Motors and other manufacturers, many now defunct, built "seedling miles" to catalyze the development of the first coast-to-coast highway in the United States.[24] And in the high-tech sector today, the competition between alternative information infrastructures—such as that between Java "applets" or UNIX programs over the Internet versus the Wintel desktop system—makes it particularly important to think about complements.

The biggest benefit of taking complementors seriously is that they add a cooperative dimension to the "competitive forces" approach. As Brandenburger and Nalebuff put it,

> Thinking [about] complements is a different way of thinking about business. It's about finding ways to make the pie bigger rather than fighting with competitors over a fixed pie. To benefit from this insight, think about how to expand the pie by developing new complements or making existing complements more affordable.[25]

In the next chapter, we will more precisely define the size of the pie that can be created by cooperating with complementors (and with other types of players). Here, we will simply stress the idea that cooperation with complementors to expand the size of the pie must be supplemented with some consideration of competition with them if the firm is to claim slices of that pie. Common sense suggests a number of heuristics that determine the extent to which complementors, as a class of players, are likely to claim the value that has been created at the expense of competitors:

- Relative concentration. Complementors are more likely to have the power to pursue their own agenda when they are concentrated relative to competitors and are less likely to be able to do so when they are relatively fragmented. Thus competitors in video games such as Nintendo have deliberately fragmented their base of complementors—independent game developers—so as to reduce their power.

- Relative buyer or supplier switching costs. When the costs to buyers or suppliers of switching across complementors are greater than their costs of switching across competitors, that increases complementors' ability to pursue their own agendas. For instance, the cost of switching the software on your desktop is likely to be significantly higher than the cost of switching your Internet service provider, with clear implications for how much of the economic pie those two classes of players can hope to capture.

- Ease of unbundling. Complements will tend to have less power if consumers can purchase and use products independently of them. For instance, applications software programs, while being complements to the manufacturers of microprocessors, tend to be less important than the operating system (e.g., Windows). Many categories of application programs can be (and are) purchased independently.

- Differences in pull-through. As complementors play a greater role in pulling through demand (e.g., through differentiation) or supply (e.g., through volumes commanded), their power is likely to expand. Thus, in the media and entertainment sector, content providers complement but also cause grave concern for several other types of players.

- Asymmetric integration threats. Complementors are likely to have more power when they can threaten to invade competitors' turf more credibly than competitors can threaten to invade the turf of the complementors.

- Rate of growth of the pie. From a behavioral perspective, competition with complementors to claim value is likely to be less intense when the size of the pie available to be divided among competitors and complementors is growing rapidly.

This list of the determinants of complementors' power could probably be lengthened. The end result is sometimes depicted as adding a "sixth force" to Porter's "five forces" framework. Nevertheless, landscape analysis should not be considered simply an extended version of the "five forces" framework for industry analysis. Both cooperative and competitive relationships must be taken into account for *all* players, regardless of the "force" under which they might be listed.

A review of the templates for landscape analysis discussed so far in this chapter—supply-demand analysis, the "five forces" framework, and the value net—suggests that one way in which each generalizes its predecessor(s) is by bringing new types of players into the analysis. The next question is obvious: Can additional improvements in our ability to understand the business landscape be achieved by further broadening the types of players considered?

The answer to that question depends on the situation under scrutiny but seems, in some cases, to be clearly affirmative. For example, it is often important to account for nonmarket relationships—such as interactions with the government, the media, activist/interest groups, and the public—that may be distinguished from market relationships by attributes such as legal specifications of due process, majority rule, broad enfranchisement, and collective action.[26] In many emerging markets, for instance, nonmarket relationships with governmental entities seem to be at least as important as market relationships in determining economic performance. Or to take another example, the "contributors" who voluntarily provide the cash that keeps many loss-making nonprofit entities in operation appear to behave very differently from suppliers of capital who are interested in the recipient's profits. Hence, in certain contexts, these relationships may need to be examined separately.

Michael Porter and others have argued that such nonmarket relationships are best accounted for by folding them into the analysis of market relationships—by looking at the role of government, for instance, solely in terms of how it affects the five (or six) forces. But, as David Baron has pointed out, the advantages of such "folding in" become less obvious when the challenge is to develop integrated strategies that explicitly address both market and nonmarket relationships.[27] It seems particularly important to separate out the government's meta-role as rule maker or regulator of interactions among other players.[28]

A simple theme should have emerged amid all of this complexity: It is impossible to specify a single, all-purpose template for analyzing the business landscape. Instead, the successively more general approaches to landscape analysis discussed so far in this chapter are valuable primarily because they remind us that we must think broadly about the other players involved and they suggest a process for doing so. The rest of this chapter focuses on that topic.

THE PROCESS OF MAPPING BUSINESS LANDSCAPES

Having reviewed the historical development of different approaches to the business landscape, it is time to discuss how managers can link such thinking to strategic planning and action. The major purpose of mapping the business landscape is *not* (as is often misunderstood) to identify whether one operates on a part of it that is high above or well below economic sea level (in the terms we used in discussing Exhibit 2.1). Instead, it is to understand the reasons for such variations and, ideally, to capitalize on them.

The first step in the process of mapping the business landscape is to draw boundaries around the part to be described in detail, by identifying the types of players that will be taken into account. The mapping process, which usually comes next, involves identifying and sometimes calibrating key relationships among the players considered. The final step is to find ways of adapting to or shaping those relationships so as to maximize a business's total profitability, rather than just the average profitability of the environment in which it operates. Although it may be necessary to cycle through these steps more than once, they are most simply considered in turn.

Step 1: Drawing the Boundaries

For most business strategy issues, zooming in on sets of players with a direct impact on the profitability of one's own business model offers more insight than reviewing the economy as a whole. Operationally, the challenge for the strategist is to decide how broadly (or narrowly) to focus in mapping the business landscape.

The industry definitions or units of analysis commonly used in the business press and by other popular information providers are, in many cases, inappropriate; they therefore need to be redrawn if they are to be helpful. For example, a strategist would split the "auto and truck" group in the Value Line classification system on which Exhibit 2.1 is based into "autos" and "trucks" at least, because buyers, competitors, and even suppliers differ across those two segments.

Official statistical definitions such as the Standard Industrial Classification (SIC) code, which has been employed in the United States since the 1930s, sometimes fare better, but not by much. For example, at the four-digit level, the U.S. SIC code distinguishes between motor vehicles and passenger cars on the one hand and trucks and buses on the other. It nevertheless raises as many questions as it resolves—for instance, it lumps light trucks together with heavy trucks, even though the former are frequently used for personal transportation.[29]

Managers tend to favor general principles for drawing boundaries that clearly define what their mapping exercise will and will not cover over any particular classification system, official or otherwise. Perhaps the most helpful principle in this regard—and certainly the one that has been emphasized the most—is implicit in the generalization from supply-demand analysis to the "five forces" framework: Important substitution possibilities must be taken into account. Thus, in addition to direct competitors that use the same suppliers and the same technology to make the same products, maps typically include indirect competitors that offer products or services that are close substitutes for those of the firm. Current and potential technological substitutability often must be taken into account as well: "Disruptive" technologies that may fulfill customers' needs in the future (but not at present) are particularly easy to overlook, and can be particularly dangerous.[30] Taken together, these considerations suggest that companies that (potentially) share customers or technologies should be incorporated into the map.[31] Thus a decision about whether it makes sense to analyze cars and light trucks as part of the same map depends on both the degree of demand-side substitutability between the two product lines and the extent to which know-how and production equipment can be cross-utilized (supply-side substitutability).

A second general principle for drawing boundaries—for deciding which sets of players to include and which ones to exclude—is implicit in the generalization from the "five forces" framework to the value net. That is, the map must take important complementarities as well as substitution possibilities into account. This inclusion does, however, complicate the picture in one respect. The same player may simultaneously enact the roles of competitor and complementor, or it may switch from one role to the other—what Brandenburger and Nalebuff deem the "Jekyll and Hyde" effect.[32] Multiple, shifting relationships of this sort add to the difficulty of landscape analysis by enriching the palette of possibilities. They also suggest the advisability of separating the identification of the players that are relevant (step 1 of the analysis) from the assessment of the relationships among them (step 2).

Players other than the types suggested by the "five forces" framework or the value net may need to be included in the analysis as well (as noted in the previous section). The challenge is to strike the appropriate balance between manageable simplicity and requisite complexity. Or, as Albert Einstein put it, the analysis should be made as simple as possible but no simpler.

At this juncture, three common pitfalls in identifying the relevant players deserve to be mentioned. First, there is often a tendency to focus on existing players, but new or potential ones must also be taken into account. Second, players need to be considered in terms of detailed subcategories rather than just the broad categories identified in the analytical templates we have discussed so far. It would be hard, for instance, to analyze the degree of threat posed by supplier relationships to integrated steel makers without recognizing that labor represents an important subcategory of suppliers. Yet classroom attempts to analyze the landscape of integrated steel using the "five forces" framework sometimes miss this point by considering only the subcategories of suppliers of physical inputs such as iron ore or electricity. Third, players need to be clearly and consistently labeled from the perspective of the business that motivates the analysis in the first place. To return to the example of integrated steel making, case discussions have sometimes confused rivals with suppliers on the grounds that rivals supply their own buyers!

Most of the remaining ambiguities in drawing boundaries revolve around various dimensions of scope:

- Horizontal—across product markets

- Vertical—along the supplier → buyer chain

- Geographic—across local, regional, and national boundaries

Horizontal Scope   The issue of horizontal scope has already been highlighted in the passenger car/light truck example. When it is unclear whether a narrow horizontal definition or a broad one makes more sense, it may be useful to analyze the landscape based on both narrow and broad definitions. A narrow definition focuses on the analysis, and the broad one helps guard against being blindsided. If differences among segments make it difficult to analyze the broader definition, then the landscape is appropriately defined narrowly. In any event, the principles of substitutability and complementarity are particularly helpful in resolving issues that relate to this particular dimension of scope.

Vertical Scope   In regard to vertical scope, the key issue is how many vertically linked stages of the supplier → buyer chain the analysis will consider. For example, can one analyze bauxite mining, alumina refining, aluminum smelting, and fabrication of aluminum products independently of one another? In general, if a competitive market for third-party sales exists between vertical stages or could be created, the stages should be uncoupled; if not, they should remain coupled. In this sense, the tightest coupling in the vertical aluminum chain occurs between bauxite mining and alumina refining, because most refineries can employ only one source of bauxite. The loosest coupling arises between aluminum smelting and fabrication, because fabricators can buy aluminum ingot from the London Exchange as well as from different smelters.

Geographic Scope   The issue here is how broadly the business landscape should be defined in geographic terms. For example, does it make more sense to look at pharmaceutical manufacturers in the United States only or the worldwide pharmaceutical industry? Such issues can arise around local and regional boundaries as well as national ones. A key criterion in settling them is the relative independence of competitive positions—the topic of the next chapter—in different geographic markets. Because of the importance of amortizing their huge research and development (R&D) expenditures, pharmaceutical manufacturers have higher interdependence across markets than do steel makers, suggesting that the pharmaceutical landscape should generally be defined to have broader geographic scope. We note, however, that the appropriate boundaries will, along this and other scope-related dimensions, depend on the strategic issue to be addressed. Thus major pharmaceutical companies might take a global perspective in deciding whether to merge with a counterpart so as to continue to clear an increasing scale-economy threshold, but would be better advised to take more of a local or a regional perspective when setting their strategies for individual country markets.

To summarize this discussion of step 1, the challenge of identifying the players that will be kept in, as opposed to left out of, deep analysis of the business landscape is a considerable one. It must, however, be faced. The principles and guidelines offered here should help in that respect.

Step 2: Mapping Key Relationships

Identification of the relevant types of players paves the way for actually mapping the relationships among them. Some relationships may turn out to be insignificant for the actual or potential performance of the business from whose perspective the analysis is being conducted. More generally, not all the potential types of players will be of equal importance in any particular situation.

The mapping process can be conducted with two very different objectives, both of which are encountered in practice (albeit rarely within the same company). One approach calibrates relationships in quantitative or categorical terms (e.g., low versus medium versus high power for one's own side) so as to yield something akin to a traditional decision support system. The other approach focuses on mental models rather than literal decision-support models, stressing that key decision makers should understand key relationships in some depth. Both approaches have succeeded in numerous practical applications, explaining why both are still practiced extensively. Also, in many situations, taking either approach is likely to be better than doing nothing. In other words, decision-support models and mental models may have a large zone of overlap within which the intelligent pursuit of either of them can improve on the organizational status quo.

Although the two approaches may seem fundamentally different, they have many of the same implications for the process of mapping relationships in terms of the kinds of information required, the range of relationships that must be considered, and the attention that must be paid to landscape dynamics.

Information Requirements   Both approaches require the acquisition and integration of a large amount of information about the external environment. This challenge is compounded by the need to assess changes in relationships over time (or across issues), a factor that usually mandates ongoing rather than one-off attempts to map business landscapes. Setting up and operating a system for more or less continuous environmental scans carries considerable fixed costs, but these costs can be spread out across the other types of analysis discussed in the chapters that follow. Many of the data required for such analysis can be obtained from public sources—see Exhibit 2.7 for a partial list of sources—although data from field interviews are often essential as well.

Cooperative and Competitive Relationships   A second procedural conclusion that is gaining ground involves the presumption that both cooperative and competitive relationships (or, more precisely, cooperative and competitive elements of relationships) should be reflected in business landscapes. Although this requirement adds to the difficulty of the analysis, it also enhances the chances of finding win-win strategies, in which the size of the economic pie expands, as opposed to focusing solely on win-lose strategies, in which the shares of a largely fixed pie are merely redistributed.

The "five forces" framework generally fails to account for cooperative relationships. The one exception, ironically, concerns relationships among direct competitors: Porter's treatment of rivalry determinants emphasizes, in keeping with classical IO, the structural determinants of competitors' ability to collude. This general inattention to cooperative relationships is one of the key reasons that many strategists have recently argued that one cannot define industries satisfactorily, particularly in the high-tech sector, and proposed a host of replacements—strategic blocs, webs, and ecosystems,[33] to name just a few. The analytical

E X H I B I T **2.7**

Public Sources of Information about the Business Landscape

Industry Studies
— Books
— Investment analysts
— Market research
— Business school cases

Trade Associations

Business Press
— General publications (e.g., *Wall Street Journal, Fortune*)
— Specialized industry trade journals
— Local newspapers
— Online services (e.g., Bloomberg, One-Source, Compustat)

Government Sources
— Antitrust, legal, or tax documents
— Census or IRS data
— Regulatory bodies

Industry and Company Directories
— *Thomas' Register*
— Dun & Bradstreet

Company Sources
— Annual reports
— SEC filings
— Public relations/promotional material
— Internet sites
— Company histories

guidelines proposed in this section do not depend on whether you choose to use newer terminology of this sort or not.

Having recognized cooperative relationships, we must remember that competitive thinking can help identify, even if only qualitatively, which types of players will tend to get how much of the economic pie that *is* created. The detailed heuristics spelled out in the "five forces" framework provide a very helpful checklist in this regard, although it usually makes sense to work through the list rather quickly and identify a few key factors to explore in depth. The version of the value net developed in the previous section also suggests that similar heuristics can usefully be applied even to relationships with complementors that are, relatively speaking, more cooperative and less competitive in nature. Tests of consistency (e.g., between predicted and reported profits) can be used to check the analysis that has been performed up to this point.

Dynamic Thinking   The final reason why attempts to map relationships among players offer both dividends and difficulties is that those relationships tend to change over time, partly as a result of the strategies adopted by various players. One obvious implication of such change is that we should map the business landscape the way it will be in the future rather than the way it was in the past. Successful prediction of how the business landscape will change can prove extremely valuable, just as a failure to anticipate changes can be disastrous.

It is useful, in this regard, to distinguish between short-run and long-run dynamics. Although short-run dynamics reflect transient effects, they also pick up on phenomena such as business cycles that can be quite important, particularly in capacity-driven industries. In the U.S. steel industry, for example, integrated steel makers' attempts to modernize were regularly and debilitatingly interrupted by cyclical downturns, which increased the profit potential for minimills.

In the longer run, attention needs to be paid to dynamics such as market growth, the evolution of buyer needs, the rate of product and process innovation, changes in the scale required to compete, changes in input costs, changes in exchange rates, and so on. Many types of long-run dynamics are possible, as Exhibit 2.8 illustrates. Some of the changes may cut across more than one set of relationships. Others may reflect long-run cycles of the sort exemplified in Exhibit 2.9. Changes may also be drastic rather than incremental. A number of contemporary forces—including advances in information technology, deregulation, and globalization—can be envisioned as subjecting a large number of landscapes, in both emerging and developed markets, to shocks or discontinuous changes that are qualitatively distinct in their competitive effects from cycles and trends.

Finally, many kinds of dynamics may be endogenous to (dependent upon) players' strategies rather than exogenously given. To help fix ideas, let's examine an example. Consider brewing, in which the minimum efficient production scale of 5 million barrels would, if divided by a U.S. market volume of approximately 200 million barrels, translate into a 2.5% market share. Yet concentration has increased steadily in the postwar period well beyond the level that would be

EXHIBIT **2.8**

Some Common Long-Run Dynamics (*Source:* Jan W. Rivkin)

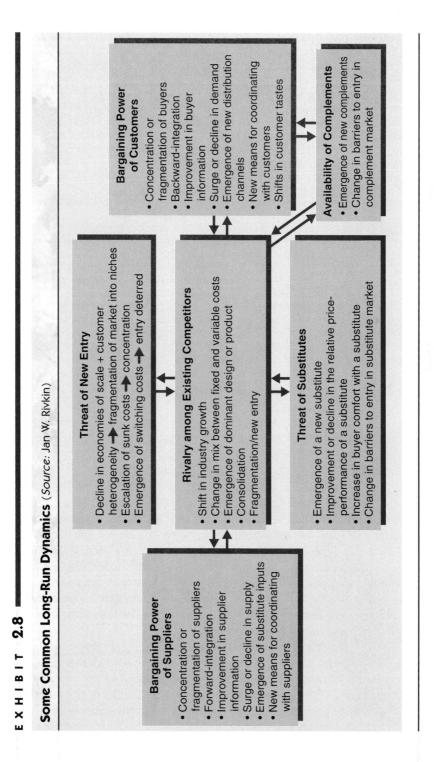

Threat of New Entry
- Decline in economies of scale + customer heterogeneity → fragmentation of market into niches
- Escalation of sunk costs → concentration
- Emergence of switching costs → entry deterred

Rivalry among Existing Competitors
- Shift in industry growth
- Change in mix between fixed and variable costs
- Emergence of dominant design or product
- Consolidation
- Fragmentation/new entry

Threat of Substitutes
- Emergence of a new substitute
- Improvement or decline in the relative price-performance of a substitute
- Increase in buyer comfort with a substitute
- Change in barriers to entry in substitute market

Bargaining Power of Customers
- Concentration or fragmentation of buyers
- Backward-integration
- Improvement in buyer information
- Surge or decline in demand
- Emergence of new distribution channels
- New means for coordinating with customers
- Shifts in customer tastes

Availability of Complements
- Emergence of new complements
- Change in barriers to entry in complement market

Bargaining Power of Suppliers
- Concentration or fragmentation of suppliers
- Forward-integration
- Improvement in supplier information
- Surge or decline in supply
- Emergence of substitute inputs
- New means for coordinating with suppliers

41

E X H I B I T   2.9

Life-Cycle Dynamics

To understand how common product life cycles are and how dramatic their effects can be, consider findings by Steven Klepper and Elizabeth Graddy. These researchers tracked 46 new products from their early history through 1981—periods covering, in some cases, nearly 100 years.[37] They found that 38 products had experienced some kind of shakeout (i.e., significant reduction in the number of producers) after periods of growth that averaged 29 years, but varied widely. Klepper and Graddy pointed out that the 8 remaining products in their sample might still be expected to contract because they were relatively young (as of 1981). Even more striking, the number of producers declined by an average of 52% from the peak for the 22 products that had achieved stability along this dimension (within 11 years of the onset of the shakeout period)!

Klepper and Graddy also found that output rose and prices fell at decreasing percentage rates over time, before stabilizing. Average *annual* changes in the first five-year interval for the products in Klepper and Graddy's sample were 50% for output and -13% for price. By the 20th to 30th years, annual changes along these dimensions had stabilized to averages, respectively, of 2% to 3% and -2% to -3%—a very sharp contrast.

The similarity across landscapes of this constellation of life-cycle related changes—and others, such as a significant shift from product R&D towards process R&D[38]—is indicative of the importance of reviving the early work on life cycles put forth by the consulting firm of Arthur D. Little and others.

implied by such calculations: The largest competitor, Anheuser-Busch, accounts for approximately 50% of the U.S. market and the second largest, Miller, for another 20%. Why?

The postwar increases in the concentration of U.S. brewing are apparently associated with increased advertising and, more generally, marketing levels. Anheuser-Busch and, to a lesser extent, Miller, appear to have pulled away from the rest of the pack by escalating their outlays along this dimension. More generally, John Sutton has used both deductive modeling and the inductive analysis of 20 food and beverage industries (including brewing) across six countries (including the United States) to argue that a profound difference separates industries with low advertising-to-sales ratios, which tend to become more fragmented as the size of the market increases, from those with high advertising-to-sales ratios, which may not become highly fragmented because they afford firms the opportunity to play escalation games.[34]

More recently, Sutton has applied similar ideas to the analysis of competition based on R&D.[35] To summarize a complex set of considerations, Sutton draws an important distinction between *exogenous sunk costs* (e.g., the costs that must be incurred to set up an efficiently scaled plant) and *endogenous sunk costs,* which denote opportunities to commit resources to (fixed) advertising and R&D outlays in ways that enhance buyers' willingness to pay to some minimal degree.[36] Sunk costs of the latter sort lend themselves to escalation games. In addition to supplying a direct example of the endogeneity of the business landscape, Sutton's work reminds us that further research may continue to change how we think about the dynamics of business landscapes and their effects on key relationships among players.

Step 3: Adapting to/Shaping the Business Landscape[39]

Having identified the key players and mapped (current and future) relationships among them, the manager's attention must turn to using that knowledge for strategic action. Landscape analysis's connection to strategic action becomes most obvious when the analysis is initially motivated by a specific choice (e.g., whether to enter or exit a particular market). Other connections to action are possible as well, however. Thus a map of the business landscape may highlight certain competitive relationships that must be countered or certain cooperative relationships that must be exploited to achieve superior economic performance, thereby reaching a high point on the landscape. Alternatively, assessment of the effects of a major change in the landscape may suggest necessary adjustments. Such adaptation of strategy to the business landscape to achieve "external fit" is a major theme of several of the strategic success cases included in this book.

For a current example of adaptation, consider the strategic actions taken by large accounting firms to mitigate the worst aspects of their business landscape. The profitability of their audit business, in particular, was being eroded by rivalry among the traditional Big Eight firms, which were similar in their sizes and in their intent of becoming the market leader, and by pressure from the typical purchaser, the Chief Financial Officer (CFO) of a client, for whom the external audit fee represented the largest item on his or her budget after salaries. Large accounting firms have responded to these pressures in a number of ways. Mergers have reduced the Big Eight to the Big Five, with further consolidation likely. The firms have also broadened the scope of their professional services (e.g., by moving into consulting) so as to shift to more attractive parts of the landscape and to increase clients' switching costs. Finally, they have attempted to shift the purchase of audit services away from CFOs and toward audit committees of clients' boards of directors, whom they perceive to be less price-sensitive.

Adaptation, while important, is not the only strategic posture that might be adopted vis-à-vis the business landscape. Our earlier discussion of the endogeneity of the business landscape suggested that a business might have the opportunity to more actively shape its environment to its own advantage—a possibility that has been headlined by a large body of recent literature that emphasizes the importance of strategic insight or foresight.[40] Opportunities to shape or reshape business landscapes are most obvious in fluid environments that are still taking form, such as multimedia, but they are also evident in older, apparently more mature contexts. Thus the automobile industry may be reshaped fundamentally by the ways in which automakers revamp their distributions systems.

Although strategies that aim to reshape business landscapes often carry high risks, the returns can be remarkable as well. For a concrete example, consider how Nintendo rebuilt the video game business in the second half of the 1980s, after sales had dropped from $3 billion in 1982 to $100 million in 1985 due to a flood of low-quality software reaching the market.[41] Exhibit 2.10 indicates that Nintendo paid attention from the very outset to setting up relationships with other players that would allow it both to grow the pie again *and* to capture a major share of the value created. We think that formal landscape analysis—thinking about who the relevant players are and how might relationships among them evolve—is more helpful in identifying successful "shaper" strategies than injunctions to be insightful.

This and other examples of successful shaper or adapter strategies also suggest a need, however, to move beyond looking at environmental attractiveness—the first of the two determinants of profitability in the profitability grid in Exhibit 1.7—to considering competitive positioning—the second of the two determinants. This move requires a shift from "industry-level" analyst to "firm-level" analysis. We can visualize this shift in landscape terms. Instead of looking at the landscape from a high altitude, where only the principal features of its various parts—such as the average height above (or below) sea level—stand out, we will zoom in for a much closer look. Our scrutiny will reveal that the landscape often looks very rugged, as in the illustration on the cover of this book. Variations in the profitability of direct competitors tend to be even larger than the common components of their profitability examined in this chapter. Understanding such differences in competitive positioning and figuring out how to create competitive advantage are the principal topics of the next chapter.

SUMMARY

Landscape analysis helps make part of the older SWOT (strengths-weaknesses-opportunities-threats) paradigm a more systematic process for strategic planning by elucidating the opportunities and threats confronting individual businesses, some of which they share with their direct competitors.

Landscape analysis is not, however, confined to direct competitors: It involves looking beyond them to an extent that depends on the generality of the analytical template employed. Supply-demand analysis focuses attention on product markets—that is, on exchange relationships between suppliers and buyers. The "five forces" framework extends the analysis (at least in principle) to three-stage (supplier → competitor → buyer) vertical chains and to explicit consideration of substitution possibilities. The value net draws complementary relationships into the picture and accounts for the complication that a player that is a competitor in one guise may be a complementor in another. Even more types of players may need to be added, depending on the context. Given the ambiguity regarding who is "in" and who is "out," achieving clarity about the participants' identities is often more important than striving for *the* right way to draw the boundaries of the portion of the business landscape that is to be mapped in detail.

EXHIBIT **2.10**

How Nintendo Reshaped the Video Game Landscape (*Source:* Unpublished analysis by Adam Brandenburger)

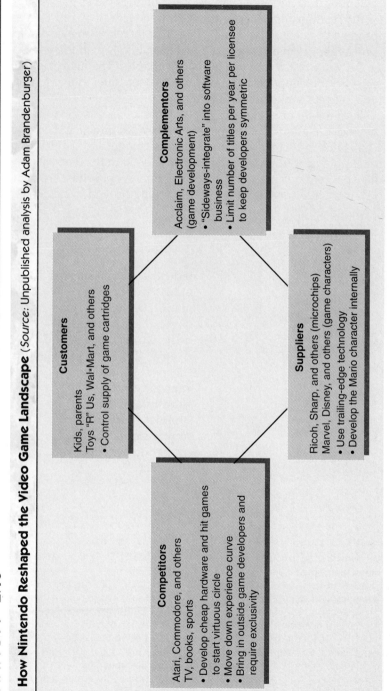

Customers

Kids, parents
Toys "R" Us, Wal•Mart, and others
• Control supply of game cartridges

Complementors

Acclaim, Electronic Arts, and others (game development)
• "Sideways-integrate" into software business
• Limit number of titles per year per licensee to keep developers symmetric

Competitors

Atari, Commodore, and others
TV, books, sports
• Develop cheap hardware and hit games to start virtuous circle
• Move down experience curve
• Bring in outside game developers and require exclusivity

Suppliers

Ricoh, Sharp, and others (microchips)
Marvel, Disney, and others (game characters)
• Use trailing-edge technology
• Develop the Mario character internally

Identification of the relevant types of players paves the way for actually mapping the relationships among them. Both cooperative and competitive relationships must be taken into account. The "five forces" framework offers a number of helpful heuristics in this regard ("the determinants of industry attractiveness"). So does the value net, as developed in this chapter. The mapping must be dynamic, because relationships can and do change over time, as a result of cycles, trends, shocks, players' strategies, and so on.

The ultimate object of such mapping exercises is to suggest ways in which businesses can adapt to or shape the landscapes in which they operate. Although the tools and principles discussed in this chapter are helpful in this regard, we must supplement them with the ones discussed in the next chapter. As the SWOT framework reminds us, perceptions of common opportunities and threats must be integrated with consideration of the strengths and weaknesses of individual players.

GLOSSARY

adaptation
business landscape
business model
buyer power
complementors
cooperation
demand curve
dynamic thinking
endogenous sunk costs
exogenous sunk costs
extended competition
external fit
"five forces" framework
geographic scope
horizontal scope

industrial organization or IO
industry definitions
nonmarket relationships
oligopolistic competition
price-elasticity of demand
rivalry
"shaper" strategies
strategic groups
substitutes
supplier power
supply curve
supply-demand analysis
value net
vertical scope

NOTES

1. This chapter has benefited enormously from the help of Adam Brandenburger and Jan Rivkin, who have developed many of the ideas that it covers, allowed us to draw on their unpublished materials, and offered comments on earlier drafts.

2. See, for example, Richard Schmalensee, "Do Markets Differ Much?", *American Economic Review,* 1984; 75:341–351; Richard Rumelt, "How Much Does Industry Matter?", *Strategic Management Journal,* 1991; 12:167–185; and Anita McGahan and Michael Porter, "How Much Does Industry Mat-

ter, Really?", *Strategic Management Journal,* 1997; 18:15–30.

3. Scott Gillis of Marakon Associates deserves our thanks for helping make these data available.

4. The landscape metaphor originated in biology more than 50 years ago. See Stuart A. Kauffman, *At Home in the Universe* (Oxford: Oxford University Press, 1995) for a discussion in that context. The last four chapters of his book also discuss applications to issues concerning human organizations. For other applications of landscape-based

models to strategy, see Daniel Levinthal, "Adaptation on Rugged Landscapes," *Management Science*, 1997; 53:934–950 and Jan W. Rivkin, "Imitation of Complex Strategies," Harvard Business School Working Paper 98-068.

5. The discussion builds on Adam Brandenburger's unpublished note, "Models of Markets" (Harvard Business School, January 1998).

6. Jurg Niehans, *A History of Economic Theory* (Baltimore: Johns Hopkins University Press, 1990), pp. 16–18.

7. Alfred Marshall, *Principles of Economics* (London: Macmillan, 1890), book 5.

8. See Gary P. Pisano, *Partners HealthCare System, Inc. (A)*, ICCH No. 696-062, for additional details. Also note that the implications of a decline in capacity utilization would be even more severe than implied by this cost curve because it includes fixed as well as variable costs in its cost base.

9. Antoine A. Cournot, *Recherches sur les Principes Mathématiques de la Théorie des Richesses* (Paris: Hachette, 1838). The rather different characterization of outcomes when duopolists set prices rather than quantities was provided by another French savant, Jean Bertrand, in his review of Cournot's book in the *Journal des Savants*, 1883 67:499–508.

10. See Edward H. Chamberlin, *Theory of Monopolistic Competition: A Reorientation of the Theory of Value* (Cambridge, MA: Harvard University Press, 1933), and Joan Robinson, *The Economics of Imperfect Competition* (London: Macmillan, 1933).

11. Economists associated with the University of Chicago generally doubted the empirical importance of this possibility—except as an artifact of regulatory distortions.

12. Mason's seminal work was "Price and Production Policies of Large-Scale Enterprise," *American Economic Review*, March 1939:61–74.

13. Joe S. Bain, "Relation of Profit Rate to Industry Concentration: American Manufacturing, 1936-1940," *Quarterly Journal of Economics*, August 1951:293–324.

14. Joe S. Bain, *Barriers to New Competition* (Cambridge, MA: Harvard University Press, 1956), p. 3.

15. See, for instance, Harvey J. Golschmid, H. Michael Mann, and J. Fred Weston, eds., *Industrial Concentration: The New Learning* (Boston: Little Brown, 1974).

16. Michael E. Porter, "Note on the Structural Analysis of Industries," ICCH No. 376-054.

17. Richard Schmalensee, "Inter-industry Studies of Structure and Performance," in Richard Schmalensee and R. D. Willig, eds., *Handbook of Industrial Organization*, vol. 2 (Amsterdam:

North-Holland, 1989). The elements in Porter's framework that are supported by Schmalensee's review of the evidence appear in bold print in Exhibit 2.5.

18. Darrell K. Rigby, "Managing the Management Tools," *Planning Review*, September–October 1994.

19. Richard E. Caves, Michael Fortunato, and Pankaj Ghemawat, "The Decline of Dominant Firms, 1905–1929," *Quarterly Journal of Economics*, 1984; 99:523–546.

20. Adam Brandenburger and Stuart W. Harborne, Jr., "Value-Based Business Strategy," *Journal of Economics and Management Strategy*, 1996; 5:5–29.

21. Even Porter is reported to have modified his "five forces" framework in ways suggested by the value net.

22. Andrew S. Grove, *Only the Paranoid Survive* (New York: Bantam Doubleday Dell, 1996), pp. 27–29.

23. For other examples of complementors, see Chapter 2 of *Co-opetition, op. cit.*, especially page 12.

24. Brandenburger and Nalebuff, *Co-opetition*, p. 12.

25. *Co-opetition, op. cit.*, pp. 14–15.

26. David P. Baron, "Integrated Strategy: Market and Nonmarket Components," *California Management Review*, 1995; 37(2), especially page 47. See David P. Baron, *Business and Its Environment* (Englewood Cliffs, NJ: Prentice-Hall, 1996) for an extended treatment of nonmarket strategies.

27. Baron, *op. cit.*

28. Adam M. Brandenburger, "Discussing Business Landscapes," Harvard Business School (February 1998).

29. In 1999, the Standard Industrial Classification will be replaced with the North American Industrial Classification System, which seems to provide a somewhat improved basis for bounding the business landscape.

30. See Clayton M. Christensen, *The Innovator's Dilemma* (Boston: Harvard Business School Press, 1997) as well as the discussion in Chapter 4 of this book.

31. Derek F. Abell, *Defining the Business* (Englewood Cliffs, NJ: Prentice-Hall, 1980).

32. Pages 28–29 of *Co-opetition*. More generally, "It's the norm for the same player to occupy multiple roles in the Value Net."

33. See, for instance, Nitin Nohria and Carlos Garcia-Pont, "Global Strategic Linkages and Industry Structure," *Strategic Management Journal*, 1991; 12:105–124; John Hagel and Arthur Armstrong, *Net Gain* (Boston: Harvard Business School Press, 1997); and James F. Moore, *The Death of Competition* (New York: HarperCollins, 1996).

34. John Sutton, *Sunk Costs and Market Structure* (Cambridge, MA: MIT Press, 1991).

35. John Sutton, *Technology and Market Structure* (Cambridge, MA: MIT Press, 1998).

36. One further caveat: The increase, if any, in unit variable costs associated with such attempts at vertical differentiation should be sufficiently small for an industry setting to exhibit escalation potential. In addition, note that Sutton does not speak directly to the question of how firms that are differently situated in the same industry compete over the strategic opportunities that are open to them. Rather, his focus is on establishing lower bounds on the concentration levels observed in equilibrium.

37. Steven Klepper and Elizabeth Graddy, "The Evolution of New Industries and the Determinants of Market Structure," *RAND Journal of Economics,* Spring 1990:27–44.

38. W. J. Abernathy and J. M. Utterback. "Patterns of Industrial Innovation," *Technology Review* 1978; 80:2–9.

39. While the basic ideas on which this subsection draws are well established, the adapter/shaper dichotomy used here and elsewhere in this book is based on recent work by the consulting firm of McKinsey & Company, as discussed at the McKinsey Strategy Forum.

40. Gary Hamel and C. K. Prahalad's *Competing for the Future* (Boston: Harvard Business School Press, 1994) is a leading example of this genre, but far from the only one. Common themes in this literature, based on a sorting effort by McKinsey & Company, include innovation, entrepreneurship, revolution, aspiration/ambition-based thinking, stretch and leverage, and leadership/vision.

41. This discussion is directly based on Adam Brandenburger's "Power Play (A): Nintendo in 8-Bit Video Games," ICCH No. 795-102, and his unpublished analysis of that case.

CHAPTER 3

Creating Competitive Advantage

Pankaj Ghemawat and Jan Rivkin

> If a man . . . make a better mousetrap than his neighbor, tho' he build his house in the woods, the world will make a path to his door.
>
> —*Ralph Waldo Emerson (attributed)*

*L*ecturing in the nineteenth century, Emerson anticipated one of the key points that strategists still stress at the end of the twentieth: Some mousetrap makers are likely to outperform others. More generally, while industry- or population-level effects have a large impact on business performance, large differences in performance also appear *within* industries. Consider, for example, two of the industries identified as outliers in terms of performance and analyzed in Chapter 2—pharmaceuticals and steel. Exhibit 3.1 unbundles the spreads between returns on equity and the costs of equity capital in these two industries, competitor by competitor. Some companies have historically earned less than their costs of capital even in the pharmaceutical industry, and others have historically created value even in the steel industry.

The structure within industries, often described in terms of "strategic groups," sheds some light on these differences in performance. Biotechnology firms have underperformed conventional pharmaceutical firms since the late 1970s—partly as a result of being in start-up mode over much of this period—while minimills, who make steel from scrap, have outperformed conventional integrated steel makers. But there is more to the story than just differences between these groups: Nucor, to take a case included in this book, has significantly outperformed most other minimills, not just integrated steel makers. A firm such as Nucor that earns superior financial returns within its industry (or its strategic group) over the long run is said to enjoy a *competitive advantage* over its rivals.

Recent research suggests that such within-industry performance differences are widespread. Indeed, within-industry differences in profitability may be larger than differences across industries.[1] Industry-level effects appear to account for 10% to 20% of the variation in business profitability, and stable within-industry effects account for 30% to 45%. (Most of the remainder can be assigned to effects that fluctuate from year to year.)

E X H I B I T   3.1

(a) Average Economic Profits in the Steel Industry, 1978–1996
(b) Average Economic Profits in the Pharmaceutical Industry, 1978–1996

(*Sources:* Compustat, Value Line, and Marakon Associates Analysis)

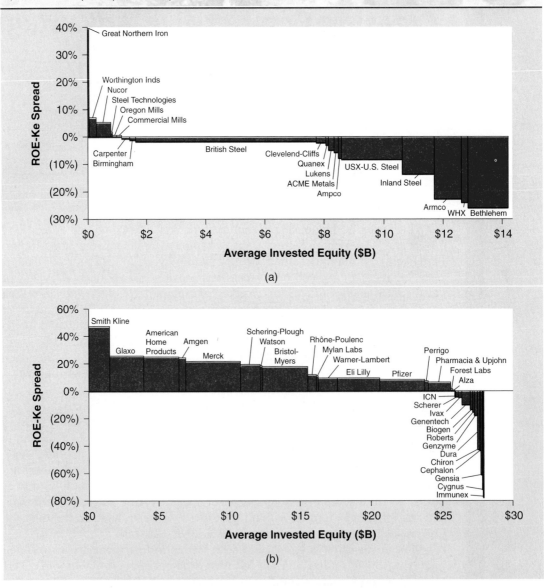

(a)

(b)

To understand such within-industry differences, we must zoom in from the industry level to look at the landscapes within industries. Examining intraindustry landscapes, which turn out to be very rugged, is the focus of this chapter. Before pursuing this goal, however, we must emphasize that such intraindustry analysis does not obviate the need for industry-level analysis. That other dimension of the profitability grid in Exhibit 1.7 also needs to be considered, in the ways described in Chapter 2, for a number of reasons.

The first reason for continuing to consider industry-level effects is that, on average, they account for a significant part of the profitability variation from business to business even if they do not account for the largest part. Second, industry-level effects may have a more persistent influence on business-level profitability than within-industry differences.[2] Third, the estimates of profitability variations cited earlier are averages that mask a great deal of variation from industry to industry. Some industries (e.g., computer leasing) "strait-jacket" firms and leave them little room to outperform the industry average; others (e.g., prepackaged software) offer more of what one might term strategic headroom.[3] Fourth, companies that beat the industry averages tend to employ strategies that successfully address the negative aspects of the structures of the industries in which they compete. Finally, market leaders, in particular, often must address the tension between managing industry structure and improving their own competitive positions within that structure. More generally, firms' competitive strategies influence industry structure as well as being influenced by it, which is why we must usually look at both.

Chapter 2 focused on industry-level effects—that is, on the common component of the profitability of direct competitors. In contrast, this chapter focuses on differences in the profits of direct competitors—that is, on the determinants of competitive advantage.[4] The first part of this chapter reviews the historical development of the core concepts included in the analysis of competitive position (either advantaged or disadvantaged): competitive cost analysis, the analysis of differentiation, cost-benefit trade-offs, and added value. The second part of this chapter draws on these concepts to lay out a process for analyzing competitive positioning, illustrated with an extended example. This tack, which is primarily analytical, is not intended to deny the importance of creativity and insight in the creation of competitive advantage. Rather, it can be read as an attempt to guide entrepreneurial energies by setting up a battery of tests for new business ideas.

THE DEVELOPMENT OF CONCEPTS FOR COMPETITIVE POSITIONING

Starting in the 1970s, traditional academic research made a number of contributions to our understanding of positioning within industries. The IO-based approach to strategic groups, initiated at the Harvard Business School by Michael Hunt's work on broadline versus narrowline strategies in the major home appliance industry, suggested that competitors within particular industries could be grouped in terms of their competitive strategies in ways that helped explain their interactions and relative profitability.[5] A stream of work at Purdue University explored the heterogeneity of competitive positions, strategies, and performance in brewing and other industries with a combination of statistical analysis and qualitative case studies.[6] More recently, *several* academic points of view have emerged about the sources of sustained performance differences within industries; these hypotheses are explored more fully in Chapter 5. The work that seems to have had the most impact on business-strategic thinking about competitive positions in the late 1970s and the 1980s, however, was more pragmatic than academic in its intent, with consultants once again playing a leading role (particularly in the development of techniques for competitive cost analysis).

Cost Analysis

With the growing acceptance of the experience curve in the 1960s, most strategists turned to some type of cost analysis as the basis for assessing competitive positions. The interest in competitive cost analysis survived the declining popularity of the experience curve in the 1970s but was reshaped by it in two important ways. First, greater attention was paid to disaggregating businesses into their components as well as to assessing how costs in a particular activity might be shared across businesses. Second, strategists greatly enriched their menu of cost drivers, expanding it beyond just experience.

The disaggregation of businesses into components was motivated, in part, by early attempts to "fix" the experience curve so as to deal with the rising real prices of many raw materials in the 1970s.[7] The proposed fix involved splitting costs into the costs of purchased materials and "cost added" (value added minus profit margins) and then redefining the experience curve as applying only to the latter category. The natural next step was to disaggregate a business's entire cost structure into parts—functions, processes, or activities—whose costs might be expected to behave in interestingly different ways. (To be consistent with later sections of this chapter, we will refer to the parts as "activities."[8]) As in the case of portfolio analysis, the idea of splitting businesses into component activities diffused quickly among consultants and their clients in the 1970s. A template for activity analysis that became especially prominent is reproduced in Exhibit 3.2.

Activity-based analysis also suggested a way of circumventing the "freestanding" conception of individual businesses built into the concept of SBUs.[9] One persistent problem in splitting diversified corporations into SBUs was that, with the exception of pure conglomerates, SBUs often shared elements of their cost structure with one another. Consulting firms—particularly Bain and Company and Strategic Planning Associates—began to emphasize the development of "field maps," or matrices that identified shared costs at the level of individual activities that were linked across businesses.[10]

In another important development in competitive cost analysis during the late 1970s and early 1980s, strategists began to consider a richer menu of cost drivers.

E X H I B I T **3.2**

McKinsey's Business System (*Source:* Carter F. Bales, P. C. Chatterjee, Donald J. Gogel, and Anupam P. Puri, "Competitive Cost Analysis," McKinsey & Co. Staff Paper (January 1980))

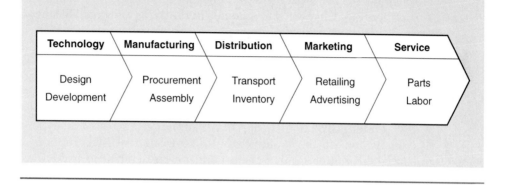

Technology	Manufacturing	Distribution	Marketing	Service
Design	Procurement	Transport	Retailing	Parts
Development	Assembly	Inventory	Advertising	Labor

Scale effects, although officially lumped into the experience curve, had long been studied independently in particular cases. Even more specific treatment of the effects of scale was now forced by activity analysis that might indicate, for example, that advertising costs were driven by national scale whereas distribution costs were driven by local or regional scale. Field maps underscored the potential importance of economies (or diseconomies) of scope across businesses rather than scale within a given business. The effects of capacity utilization on costs, for example, were dramatized by macroeconomic downturns in the wake of the two oil shocks. The globalization of competition in many industries highlighted the location of activities as a key driver of competitors' cost positions, and so on. Cost drivers are discussed more comprehensively in the second major section of this chapter.

Differentiation Analysis

Increasingly sophisticated cost analysis was followed, with a relatively large lag, by greater attention being paid to customers in the process of analyzing competitive position. Of course, customers had never been entirely invisible: Even in the heyday of experience curve analysis, market segmentation had been an essential strategic tool—although it was sometimes used to gerrymander markets to "demonstrate" a positive link between share and cost advantage rather than for a truly analytical purpose. By one insider's recollection (that of Walker Lewis, the founder of Strategic Planning Associates), "To those who defended the classic experience-curve strategy, about 80 percent of the businesses in the world were commodities."[11] In the 1970s, this view began to change.

As strategists paid more attention to customer analysis, they began to reconsider the idea that attaining low costs and offering customers low prices was always the best way to compete. Instead, they focused more closely on *differenti-*

ated ways of competing that might let a business command a price premium by improving customers' performance or reducing their (other) costs.[12] Although (product) differentiation had always occupied center stage in marketing, the idea of considering it in a cross-functional, competitive context that also accounted for cost levels apparently started to emerge in business strategy in the 1970s. Thus one member of Harvard's Business Policy group assigned Joe Bain's writings on entry barriers (see Chapter 2) to students in the 1970s and recalls using the concepts of cost and differentiation—implicit in two of Bain's three sources of entry barriers—to organize classroom discussions.[13] McKinsey began to apply the distinction between cost and "value" in its consulting activities later in the same decade.[14] The first extensive treatments of cost *and* differentiation, in Michael Porter's *Competitive Strategy* and in a *Harvard Business Review* article by William Hall, appeared in 1980.[15]

Porter's 1985 book, *Competitive Advantage,* suggested analyzing cost and differentiation via the "value chain," a template that is reproduced in Exhibit 3.3. Although Porter's value chain bore some resemblance to McKinsey's business system, his discussion of this construct emphasized the importance of regrouping functions into the activities actually performed to produce, market, deliver, and support products, thinking about linkages among activities, and connecting the value chain to the determinants of competitive position in a specific way:

> Competitive advantage cannot be understood by looking at a firm as a whole. It stems from the many discrete activities a firm performs in designing, producing, marketing, delivering, and supporting its product. Each of these activities can contribute to a firm's relative cost position and create a basis for differentiation. The value chain disaggregates a firm into its strategically relevant activities in order to understand the behavior of costs and the existing and potential sources of differentiation.[16]

Exhibit 3.3 illustrates the value chain for an Internet start-up that sells and distributes music.

Subsequent advances in the integration of cost analysis and differentiation analysis derived not only from disaggregating businesses into activities (or processes), but also from splitting customers into segments based on cost-to-serve as well as customer needs. Such "deaveraging" of customers was often said to expose situations in which 20% of a business's customers accounted for more than 80% (or even 100%) of its profits.[17] It also suggested new customer segmentation criteria. Starting in the late 1980s, Bain & Company built a thriving "customer retention" practice based on the generally higher costs of capturing new customers as opposed to retaining existing ones.

Costs versus Differentiation

Porter and Hall, the first two strategists to write about both cost and differentiation, argued that successful companies usually had to choose to compete *either* on the basis of low costs *or* by differentiating products through quality and perfor-

E X H I B I T   3.3 ▬▬▬▬▬▬▬▬▬▬▬▬▬▬▬▬▬▬▬

Value Chain for an Internet Start-Up

Firm infrastructure	Financing, legal support, accounting					Support activities
Human Resources	Recruiting, training, incentive system, employee feedback					
Technology Development	Inventory system	Site software	Pick and pack procedures	Site look and feel Customer research	Return procedures	
Procurement	CDs Shipping	Computers Telecom lines	Shipping services	Media		
	Inbound shipment of top titles Warehousing	Server operations Billing Collections	Picking and shipment of top titles from warehouse Shipment of other titles from third-party distributors	Pricing Promotions Advertising Product information and reviews Affiliations with other Web sites	Returned items Customer feedback	Primary activities
	Inbound Logistics	Operations	Outbound Logistics	Marketing and Sales	Service	

mance characteristics. Porter popularized this idea in terms of the "generic" strategies of low cost and differentiation. He also identified a "focus" option that cut across the two basic generic strategies (see Exhibit 3.4), linking these strategic options to his work on industry analysis:

> In some industries, there are no opportunities for focus or differentiation—it's solely a cost game—and this is true in a number of bulk commodities. In other industries, cost is relatively unimportant because of buyer and product characteristics.[18]

The generic strategies appealed to strategists for at least two reasons. First, they captured a common tension between cost and differentiation: Often, a firm must incur higher costs to deliver a product or service for which customers are willing to pay more. Most customers are willing to pay more for a Toyota automobile than for a Hyundai, for example, but the costs of manufacturing a Toyota are significantly higher than the costs of making a Hyundai. Toyota's slightly higher profit margins derive from the fact that the price premium Toyota can command is slightly greater than the incremental costs associated with its product.

E X H I B I T   3.4 ━━━━━━━━

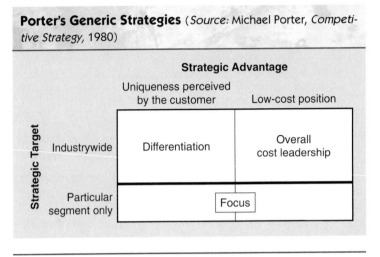

Porter's Generic Strategies (*Source:* Michael Porter, *Competitive Strategy*, 1980)

		Strategic Advantage	
		Uniqueness perceived by the customer	Low-cost position
Strategic Target	Industrywide	Differentiation	Overall cost leadership
	Particular segment only	Focus	

Second, the generic strategies were appealing because the capabilities, organizational structure, reward system, corporate culture, and leadership style needed to make a low-cost strategy succeed are, at first blush, contrary to those required for differentiation. For the sake of internal consistency and to ensure that it maintains a single-minded purpose, a firm might have to choose to compete either one way or the other.

Despite their appeal, the generic strategies provoked a vigorous debate among strategists, for both empirical and logical reasons. Empirically, the tension between cost and differentiation does not appear absolute: Firms *can* discover ways to produce superior products at lower costs. In the 1970s and 1980s, for instance, Japanese manufacturers in a number of industries found that, by reducing defect rates, they could make higher quality products at lower cost. Until recently, McDonald's brand recognition and product consistency permitted it to charge a slight premium over competing fast-food vendors, even though its national scale, franchisee relationships, and rigorous standardization allowed it to incur lower costs than its rivals.[19] Such eye-catching examples of dual competitive advantage seemed to refute the idea of generic strategies.[20] Exhibit 3.5 traces the interplay between cost and differentiation in an expanded treatment of competitive advantage that recognizes the possibility of dual advantages.

How common are companies with dual competitive advantages? Porter has argued that dual advantages are rare, typically being based on operational differences across firms that are easily copied.[21] Others contend that rejecting the trade-offs between cost and differentiation—replacing trade-offs with "trade-ons"—represents a fundamental way to transform competition in an industry.[22] The debate continues today.

A second challenge to the notion of generic strategies is logical in nature. Although a desire for internal consistency may drive companies to the extremes of

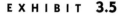

E X H I B I T   3.5

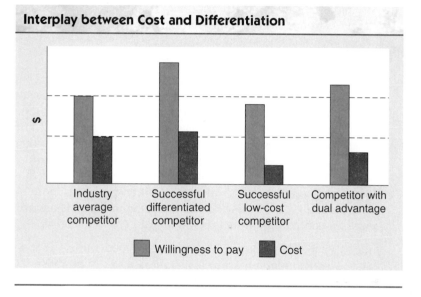

Interplay between Cost and Differentiation

$

Industry average competitor | Successful differentiated competitor | Successful low-cost competitor | Competitor with dual advantage

■ Willingness to pay   ■ Cost

low cost and high differentiation, external considerations may pull firms back toward the center. If most customers want neither the simplest nor the most elaborate product, for instance, the most profitable strategy may be to offer a product of moderate quality and to incur moderate costs. In apparel retailing in the United Kingdom, for example, Marks and Spencer commands neither the highest price premium nor the lowest cost position. By selling very good (but not the best) apparel to British customers and by establishing a good (but not the lowest) cost position, Marks and Spencer has become one of the most profitable retailers—and one of the most admired companies—in the United Kingdom.[23]

In the 1990s, the general consensus among strategists, though one that falls somewhat short of being universal, does not emphasize generic strategies (Porter's or anybody else's). Instead, it embraces the idea that competitive position must consider both relative cost and differentiation, and it recognizes the tension between the two. Positioning, in this view, is an effort to drive the largest possible wedge between cost and differentiation (or price). As differentiation rises, so, too, does cost in most instances; the largest gap between the two, however, need not occur at the extremes of low costs or high price premia. The optimal position represents a choice from a spectrum of trade-offs between cost and differentiation rather than a choice between mutually exclusive generic strategies.[24]

A few examples will help illustrate the richness of positioning possibilities:

• In providing premier investment banking services to its elite list of clients, Goldman Sachs incurs higher costs than many of its competitors.[25] For instance, the company devotes considerable extra resources to maintaining its relationships with senior executives of client companies and to coordinating the services it provides to each client. As a consequence, clients are willing to pay higher fees to Goldman or, given equal fees, will choose Goldman over the competition. The premium that the firm commands is larger than the extra costs it incurs. Its pretax return on equity in 1996, 48%, far exceeded those of Merrill Lynch (20%) and Morgan Stanley (17%).

- Enterprise Rent-a-Car has configured itself to serve the rental customer whose car is in the shop. In contrast to rivals Hertz and Avis, it does not target the air traveler. Enterprise keeps its costs extremely low: It stores its fleet of cars in suburban lots rather than expensive airport facilities, it minimizes national advertising, it keeps vehicles in service six months longer than other rental companies, and so forth. As reflected by its hefty 30% price discount, customers are willing to pay less for Enterprise's services than those of Hertz or Avis. The savings from its various activities, however, more than match the price discount. As a result, an adage has emerged: "There are two types of rental car companies: those that lose money and Enterprise." [26]

- International Dairy Queen franchises fast-food outlets that feature dessert items. Thanks in large part to a sustained effort to establish its brand name, Dairy Queen can charge a 5% to 10% premium over direct competitors in its rural and suburban locations. It charges considerably less than dessert retailers, such as Haagen Dazs, that operate outlets located in shopping malls, but it also avoids the rents associated with mall locations. With customers' higher willingness to pay for its products than those offered by its rural and suburban competitors and lower costs than mall retailers, Dairy Queen has earned superior returns. Its return on equity has averaged nearly 28% over the past decade (although sustaining such high returns has proved to be a challenge in recent years).

Added Value

In the mid-1990s, Adam Brandenburger and Gus Stuart added rigor to the idea of driving the largest possible wedge between costs and differentiation through their characterization of *added value*.[27] The two considered three-stage vertical chains (suppliers → competitors → buyers) and were precise about the monetary quantities of interest. On the demand side, they mapped differentiation into buyer willingness to pay for products or services; on the supply side, they used the exactly symmetric notion of supplier opportunity costs (the smallest amounts that suppliers would accept for the services and resources required to produce specific inputs). Given these definitions, the total *value* created by a transaction is the difference between the customer's willingness to pay and the supplier's opportunity cost. The division of this value among the three levels of the vertical chain is, in general, indeterminate. Nevertheless, one upper bound on the value captured by any player equals its added value—that is, the maximal value created by all participants in the vertical chain minus the maximal value that would be created without that particular player.

More precisely, the amount of value that a firm can claim cannot exceed its added value under *unrestricted bargaining*. To see why this constraint applies, assume for a moment that a lucky firm *does* strike a deal that allows it to capture more than its added value. The value left over for the remaining participants is then less than the value that they could generate by arranging a deal among themselves. The remaining participants could, after all, break off and form a separate pact that improves their collective lot. Any deal that grants a firm more than its added value is vulnerable to such breakaway possibilities.

For an illustration of the usefulness of this style of analysis, consider the ill-starred decision by the Holland Sweetener Company (HSC) to enter the aspartame industry in late 1986, when it was monopolized by NutraSweet.[28] HSC's costs were probably higher, even after its initial capital investment was sunk, than those of NutraSweet because of limited scale and learning. In addition, customers' willingness to pay for HSC's aspartame was probably lower because of NutraSweet's heavy investments in building up its brand identity. HSC decided to enter the market anyway, presumably because the prices that Coca-Cola and Pepsi-Cola were paying NutraSweet were approximately three times as high as HSC's prospective costs.

As things turned out, the big winners from HSC's entry were Coke and Pepsi, which were able to extract much lower prices from NutraSweet. An explanation of this development is suggested in Exhibit 3.6, which graphs in stylized terms the willingness to pay and the relevant costs post-entry. Evidently, HSC's entry depressed NutraSweet's added value (hence the lower prices). HSC, however, could not expect to have added value post-entry (given unrestricted bargaining)

E X H I B I T 3.6

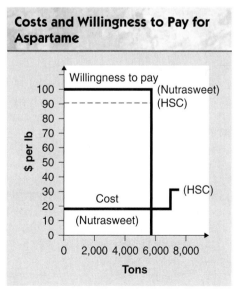

Costs and Willingness to Pay for Aspartame

because total value created would not be reduced if the firm were to disappear.[29] So HSC had to do something more if it wanted to enter this business profitably, beyond simply jumping in. One possibility would have been to convince Coke and Pepsi to pay it to play up front, instead of relying on their "goodwill" after its entry to amortize its fixed costs.[30] Another approach would have been to communicate that HSC's market share goals were sufficiently modest that it made no sense for NutraSweet, to the extent that the incumbent had some discretion, to lower its own prices across the board.[31]

Added value can sometimes be calculated, as was approximately the case in the context of aspartame. Even when it cannot, however, it provides a useful heuristic for judging a firm's strategy: If a firm were to disappear, would someone in its network of suppliers, customers, and complementors miss it? This question is harder-edged than older heuristics in the same vein—come up with a better product (à la Emerson), manage for uniqueness, focus on your distinctive competence, and so on—because it is based on an explicit model of interactions among buyers, suppliers, competitors, and complementors. This model also supplies a particularly interesting benchmark.

The concept of added value also helps tie together intraindustry analysis of competitive advantage and industry-level analysis of average profitability as well. In an industry with an "unattractive" structure, competitors' added values tend to be low, with exceptions arising only in the case of firms that have managed to create competitive advantages for themselves—that is, driven bigger wedges than most of their competitors between buyers' willingness to pay and costs. In more "attractive" industries, a firm may expect to do better than its competitive advantage alone would guarantee, through two mechanisms. First, the added values of individual competitors tend to be larger than their competitive advantages in such industry environments. Second, some such industries seem to make it feasible for competitors to engage in what is politely termed "recognition of mutual dependence" and is less politely described as "tacit collusion" (an important determinant of the degree of rivalry and an important departure from the assumption of unrestricted bargaining).

A PROCESS FOR ANALYSIS[32]

Having reviewed the historical development of concepts for competitive positioning, we now discuss a process for linking such concepts to strategic planning and action. How can managers identify opportunities to raise willingness to pay by more than costs or to drive down costs without sacrificing too much willingness to pay? Sheer entrepreneurial insight certainly plays a large role in spotting such arbitrage opportunities. Michael Dell, for example, might see that customers are becoming comfortable with computer technology, realize that retail sales channels add more costs than benefits for many customers, and act on his insight to start a direct-to-the-customer computer business.[33] Likewise, a company such as Liz

Claiborne might perceive a huge pent-up demand for a collection of medium- to high-end work clothes for female professionals.[34] Dumb luck also plays a role. Engineers searching for a coating material for missiles in the 1950s discovered the lubricant WD-40, whose sales continue to earn a return on equity between 40% and 50% four decades later.

We believe, however, that smart luck beats dumb luck and that analysis can hone insight. To analyze competitive advantage, strategists typically break a firm down into discrete activities or processes and then examine how each contributes to the firm's relative cost position or comparative willingness to pay.[35] The activities undertaken to design, produce, sell, deliver, and service goods are what ultimately incur costs and generate customer willingness to pay. Differences across firms in activities—differences in what firms actually do on a day-to-day basis—produce disparities in cost and willingness to pay and hence dictate added value. By analyzing a firm, activity by activity, managers can (1) understand why the firm does or does not have added value, (2) spot opportunities to improve a firm's added value, and (3) foresee future shifts in added value.

The starting point of positioning analysis is usually to catalog a business's activities. We can often facilitate the task of grouping the myriad activities that a business performs into a limited number of economically meaningful categories by referring to generic templates for activity analysis, such as the ones reproduced in Exhibits 3.2 and 3.3. Porter's value chain, which distinguishes between primary activities that directly generate a product or service and support activities that make the primary activities possible, is particularly helpful in ensuring that one considers a comprehensive array of activities. Generic templates cannot, however, be used blindly, for two reasons. First, not all of the activities they identify will be relevant in any particular situation. Second, data often come prepackaged so as to favor a particular way of cataloging activities—unless a major effort to "clean up" such data is deemed necessary.

The rest of the analysis usually proceeds in three steps. First, managers examine the costs associated with each activity, using differences in activities to understand how and why their costs differ from those of competitors. Second, they analyze how each activity generates customer willingness to pay, studying differences in activities to see how and why customers are willing to pay more or less for the goods or services of rivals. Finally, managers consider changes in the firm's activities, with the objective of identifying changes that will widen the wedge between costs and willingness to pay.

The following subsections discuss these steps in this order, although it is often necessary to iterate back and forth among them in practice. To illustrate their application, we focus on a simple example: the snack cake market in the western region of Canada.[36] Between 1990 and 1995, Little Debbie grew its share of this market from 1% to nearly 20%. At the same time, Hostess, the maker of such long-time favorites as Twinkies and Devil Dogs, saw its dominant 45% share dwindle to 25%. An analysis of competitive positioning shows why Little Debbie and Hostess fared so differently and helps suggest a strategy for the latter.

Step 1: Using Activities to Analyze Relative Costs

Typically, competitive cost analysis is the starting point for the strategic analysis of competitive advantage. In pure commodity businesses, such as wheat farming, customers refuse to pay a premium for any company's product. In this type of setting, a low-cost position is the key to added value and competitive advantage. Even in industries that are not pure commodities, however, differences in cost often exert a large influence on differences in profitability.

To begin with our example, in the early 1990s, Hostess's managers struggled to understand why their financial performance was poor and their market share was plummeting. They cataloged the major elements of their value chain and calculated the costs associated with each class of activities. As Exhibit 3.7 shows, although Hostess sold the typical package of snack cakes to retailers for 72¢, raw materials (ingredients and packaging material) accounted for only 18¢ per unit. Operation of automated baking, filling, and packaging production lines (largely depreciation, maintenance, and labor costs) amounted to 15¢. Outbound logistics—delivery of fresh goods directly to convenience stores and supermarkets, and maintenance of shelf space—constituted the largest portion of costs, 26¢. Marketing expenditures on advertising and promotions added another 12¢. Thus a mere penny remained as profits for Hostess.

After calculating the costs associated with each activity, the managers then determined the set of cost drivers associated with each activity. *Cost drivers* are the factors that make the cost of an activity rise or fall. For instance, the Hostess managers realized that the cost of outbound logistics per snack cake fell rapidly as a firm increased its local market share, because delivery costs depended largely on

E X H I B I T   3.7

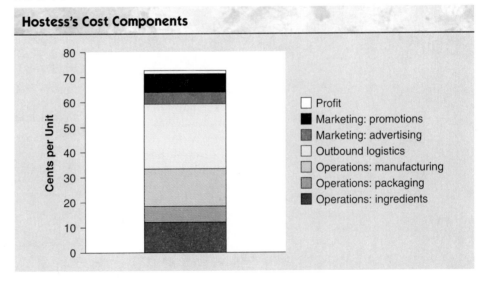

Hostess's Cost Components

the number of stops that a truck driver had to make. Thus, the larger was a firm's market share, the greater was the number of snack cakes a driver could deliver per stop. Urban deliveries tended to be more expensive than suburban ones, because city traffic slowed down drivers. Outbound logistics costs also rose with product variety: A broad product line made it difficult for drivers to restock shelves and remove out-of-date merchandise. Finally, the nature of the product itself affected logistics costs. For instance, snack cakes with more preservatives could be delivered less frequently. Using this information, the managers developed numerical relationships between activity costs and drivers for outbound logistics activities and for the other activities depicted in Exhibit 3.7.

Cost drivers are critical because they allow managers to estimate *competitors'* cost positions. Although one usually cannot observe a competitor's costs directly, it is often possible to study such drivers. One can see, for instance, a competitor's market share, the portion of its sales in urban areas, the breadth of its product line, and the ingredients in its products. Using its own costs and the numerical relationships to cost drivers, a management team can then estimate a competitor's cost position.

The results of the cost analysis were sobering to Hostess's managers. Because Little Debbie used inexpensive raw material, purchased in bulk, and tapped national scale economies, its operations costs totaled 21¢, compared with 33¢ for Hostess. Little Debbie packed its product with preservatives so that deliveries could be made less frequently, kept its product line very simple, and benefited from growing market share. Consequently, its logistics costs per unit were less than half those of Hostess. Also, Little Debbie did not run promotions. Altogether, the managers estimated, a package of Little Debbie snack cakes cost only 34¢ to produce, deliver, and market. Exhibit 3.8 illustrates the results of the cost analysis of Hostess and its major competitors. (The comparison with the two other major competitors, Ontario Baking and Savory Pastries, was not so discouraging. Indeed, Hostess had a small cost advantage over each.)

This specific example illustrates a number of general points about relative cost analysis:[37]

- Managers often examine *actual* costs, rather than opportunity costs, because data on actual costs are concrete and available. Although the symmetric treatment of suppliers and buyers in the formalization of added value is useful—reminding us that competitive advantage can come from better management of supplier relations, rather than solely just from a focus on downstream customers—supplier opportunity costs and actual costs are usually assumed to track one another closely. Obviously, this assumption should be relaxed when it doesn't make sense.

- When reviewing a relative cost analysis, it is important to focus on differences in individual activities, not just differences in total cost. Ontario Baking and Savory Pastries, for instance, had similar total costs per unit. The two firms had different cost structures, however, and, as we will discuss later, these differences reflected distinct competitive positions.

E X H I B I T   3.8

Relative Cost Analysis

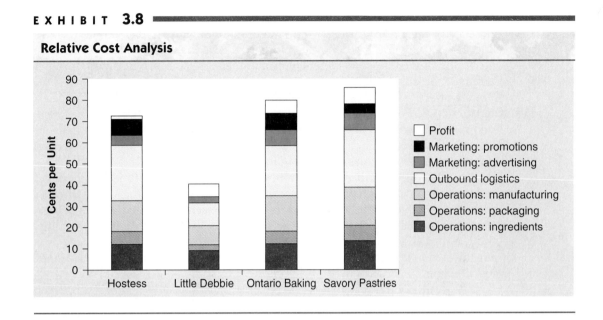

- Good cost analyses typically focus on a subset of a firm's activities. The cost analysis in Exhibit 3.8, for example, does not cover all activities in the snack cake value chain. Effective cost analyses usually break out in greatest detail and pay the most attention to cost categories that (1) pick up on significant differences across competitors or strategic options, (2) correspond to technically separable activities, or (3) are large enough to influence the overall cost position to a significant extent.

- Activities that account for a larger proportion of costs deserve more in-depth treatment in terms of cost drivers. For instance, the snack cake managers assigned several cost drivers to outbound logistics and explored these drivers in depth. They gave less attention to the drivers of advertising costs. The analysis of any cost category should focus on the drivers that have a major impact on it.

- A particular driver should be modeled only if it is likely to vary across the competitors or in terms of the strategic options that will be considered. In the snack cake example, manufacturing location influenced wages, rates, and therefore, operational costs. All of the rivals had plants in western Canada, however, and manufacturing elsewhere was not an option because shipping was costly and goods had to be delivered quickly. Consequently, manufacturing location was not considered as a cost driver.

- Finally, because the analysis of relative costs inevitably involves a large number of assumptions, sensitivity analysis is crucial. Sensitivity analysis identifies which assumptions really matter and therefore need to be honed. It also tells the analyst how confident he or she can be in the results. Under any reasonable variation of the assumptions, Little Debbie had a substantial cost advantage over Hostess.

A number of references discuss cost drivers in greater detail and suggest specific ways to model them numerically.[38] The catalog of potential drivers is long. Many relate to the size of the firm—for example, economies of scale, economies of experience, economies of scope, and capacity utilization. Others relate to differences in firm location, functional policies, timing (e.g., first-mover advantages), institutional factors such as unionization, and government regulations such as tariffs. Differences in the *resources* possessed by a firm may also drive differences in activity costs. A farm with more productive soil, for instance, will incur lower fertilization costs.

A number of pitfalls commonly snare newcomers to cost analysis. Many companies—particularly ones that produce large numbers of distinct products in a single facility—have grossly inadequate costing systems that must be cleaned up before they can be used as reference points for estimating competitors' costs. As pointed out in courses on management accounting, conventional accounting systems often overemphasize manufacturing costs and allocate overhead and other indirect costs only poorly. As firms move toward selling services and transacting on the basis of knowledge, these outdated systems will make it increasingly more difficult to analyze costs intelligently. Also problematic is a tendency to compare costs as a percentage of sales rather than in absolute dollar terms, which mixes up cost and price differences. Another common but dangerous practice is to mix together recurring costs and one-time investments. Analysts sometimes confuse differences in firms' costs with differences in their product mixes, though one can avoid this problem by comparing the cost positions of comparable products; for example, one should compare Ford's four-cylinder, mid-sized family sedan to Toyota's four-cylinder, mid-sized family sedan, rather than some imaginary "average" Ford to some "average" Toyota. Finally, a focus on costs should not crowd out consideration of customer willingness to pay—the topic of the next section.

Step 2: Using Activities to Analyze Relative Willingness to Pay

The activities of a firm do not just generate costs. They also (one hopes) make customers willing to pay for the firm's product or service. Differences in activities account for differences in willingness to pay and subsequently for differences in added value and profitability. In fact, differences in willingness to pay apparently account for more of the variation in profitability observed among competitors than do disparities in cost levels.[39]

Virtually any activity in the value chain can affect customers' willingness to pay for a product.[40] Most obviously, the product design and manufacturing activities that influence product characteristics—quality, performance, features, aesthetics—affect willingness to pay. For example, consumers pay a premium for

New Balance athletic shoes in part because the firm offers durable shoes in hard-to-find sizes. More subtly, a firm can boost willingness to pay through activities associated with sales or delivery—that is, via the ease of purchase, speed of delivery, availability and terms of credit, convenience of the seller, quality of presale advice, and so on. The catalog florist Calyx and Corolla, for instance, can command a premium because it delivers flowers faster and fresher than most of its competitors do.[41] Activities associated with post-sale service or complementary goods—customer training, consulting services, spare parts, product warranties, repair service, compatible products—also affect willingness to pay. For example, U.S. consumers may hesitate to buy a Fiat automobile because they fear that spare parts and service will be difficult to obtain. Signals conveyed through advertising, packaging, and branding efforts play a role in determining willingness to pay as well. Nike's advertising and endorsement activities, for instance, affect the premium it commands. Finally, support activities can have a surprisingly large, if indirect, impact on willingness to pay. Thus, the hiring, training, and compensation practices of Nordstrom create a helpful, outgoing sales staff that permits the department store to charge a premium for its clothes.

Ideally, a company would like to have a "willingness-to-pay calculator"—something that indicates how much customers would pay for any combination of activities. For a host of reasons, however, such a calculator usually remains beyond a firm's grasp. In many cases, willingness to pay depends heavily on intangible factors and perceptions that are hard to measure. Moreover, activities can affect willingness to pay in complicated (i.e., nonlinear and nonadditive) ways. Finally, when a business sells to end-users through intermediaries rather than directly, willingness to pay depends on multiple parties.

Lacking a truly accurate calculator, most managers use simplified methods to analyze relative willingness to pay. A typical procedure is as follows. First, managers think carefully about who the *real* buyer is. This determination can be tricky. In the market for snack cakes, for instance, the immediate purchaser is a supermarket or convenience store executive. The ultimate consumer is typically a hungry school-age child. The pivotal decision maker, however, is probably the parent who chooses among the brands.

Second, managers work to understand what the buyer or buyers want. The snack-cake-buying parent, for example, makes a purchase based on price, brand image, freshness, product variety, and the number of servings per box.[42] The supermarket or convenience store executive selects a snack cake on the basis of trade margins, turnover, reliability of delivery, consumer recognition, merchandising support, and so forth. Marketing courses discuss ways to flush out such customer needs and desires through formal or informal market research.[43] It is important that such research identifies not only what customers *want*, but also what they *are willing to pay for*. Moreover, it should reveal the most important needs for consumers and determine how customers make trade-offs among these different needs.

Third, managers assess how successful the firm and its competitors are at fulfilling customer needs. Exhibit 3.9 shows such an analysis for the snack cake mar-

EXHIBIT 3.9

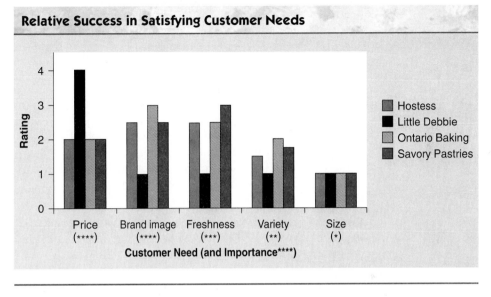

Relative Success in Satisfying Customer Needs

ket, which helps us understand both the statics and the dynamics of the market-place. Little Debbie stands out on an attribute that customers value highly (low price), while Hostess is not superior on any of the customer needs. This sort of analysis helps explain the large shifts in market share. Ontario Baking enjoys the best brand image—a position for which it has paid via relatively heavy advertising and promotion. Savory Pastries delivers the freshest product, as reflected in its high manufacturing and raw materials cost. Further analysis (not carried out in the snack cake example) can actually assign dollar values to the various customer needs. For example, it can estimate how much a customer will pay for a product that is one day fresher.

Fourth, managers relate differences in success in meeting customer needs back to company activities. Savory Pastries' high score on the freshness need, for instance, can be tied directly to specific activities regarding procurement and selection of ingredients, manufacturing, and delivery.

At this point, managers should have a refined idea of how activities translate, through customer needs, into willingness to pay. They should also understand how activities alter costs. Now they are prepared to take the final step—the analysis of different strategic options. Before moving on to that step, however, we should highlight some guidelines concerning the analysis of willingness to pay.

A major challenge in analyzing willingness to pay is narrowing the long list of customer needs down to a manageable roster. In general, we can ignore needs that have little bearing on customer choice. Likewise, needs that are equally well satisfied by all current and contemplated products can usually be neglected. If the group of competing products plays a small role in satisfying a need relative to other products outside the group, the need can often be removed from the list as well.

So far, we have treated all customers as being identical. In reality, of course, buyers differ in what they want and how badly they want it. Some customers in a bookstore want romance novels, while others look for business books. (This type of disparity, in which different customers rank products differently, is known as *horizontal differentiation*.) Among those customers who want Toni Morrison's new novel, some will pay for the more expensive hardback edition sooner, while others are content to wait for the less expensive soft-cover version. (*Vertical differentiation* arises when customers agree on which product is better—the hardback edition, in this example—but differ in how much they will pay for the better product.)

The analysis of willingness to pay becomes trickier, but more interesting, when customers are either horizontally or vertically differentiated. The usual response is *segmentation:* One first finds clumps of customers who share preferences and then analyzes willingness to pay on a segment-by-segment basis. In our experience, firms that identify segments tend to pinpoint between 2 and 12 clusters of customers. Diversity in customer needs and ease in customizing the firm's product or service typically increase with the number of segments that the analysis considers. Some observers have even argued that companies should move beyond segmentation to embrace *mass customization*.[44] In this approach, enabled by information and production technologies, companies begin to tailor their products to individual customers. Levi Strauss, for instance, is exploring the possibility of producing customized jeans. A customer would go to a Levi's store, have his or her measurements taken and transmitted to the factory, and receive a personalized pair of jeans in a direct-to-home shipment.

Finally, we want to emphasize the limits to analyzing willingness to pay. In some settings, it is possible to quantify willingness to pay quite precisely. For example, when a firm provides an industrial good that saves its customers a well-understood amount of money, it is relatively easy to calculate this amount. Calculations become much more difficult, however, when buyer choice includes a large subjective component, when customer tastes are evolving rapidly, and when the benefits that the customer derives from the product are hard to quantify. A wide range of market research techniques—such as surveys, hedonic pricing, attribute ratings, and conjoint analysis—have been designed to overcome such problems. Nevertheless, we remain wary especially when market research asks people to assess their willingness to pay for new products that they have never seen or for the satisfaction of needs that they themselves may not recognize. Fine market research "proved" that telephone answering machines would sell poorly, for instance.[45] In some settings, creative insight may have to replace analysis. In all settings, analysis should serve to hone insight, and not to displace it.

Step 3: Exploring Different Strategic Options and Making Choices

The final step in the analysis of cost and willingness to pay involves the search for ways to widen the wedge between the two. To this point, the management team has researched how changes in activities will affect added value. The goal now is to find favorable options. Because the generation of options is ultimately a creative act, it is difficult to lay down many guidelines for it. We can, however, suggest a few patterns from past experience:

1. It is often helpful to distill the essence of what drives each competitor. Little Debbie, for instance, saw that preservatives could substitute for fast delivery. By adding preservatives to its physical product, the company was able to reduce its delivery costs substantially. This approach also reduced customers' willingness to pay, but the reduction was smaller than the corresponding cost savings. Such distillation often suggests new ways to drive wedges between costs and willingness to pay. Savory Pastries, for instance, was tapping a willingness to pay for freshness. The Hostess managers, however, felt that Savory was not exploiting this customer need fully; a product even fresher than that available from Savory might command a large premium, which might serve as the basis for substantial added value.

2. When considering changes in activities, it is crucial to consider competitor reactions. In the snack cake example, Hostess's managers felt that Little Debbie would readily launch a price war against any competitor that tried to match its low-cost, low-price position. They were less concerned about an aggressive response from Savory Pastries, whose managers were distracted by an expansion into a different business. Competitive reactions and, more generally, competitive dynamics, are the topic of the next chapter.

3. Managers often tend to fixate on a few product characteristics and think too narrowly about benefits to buyers. They rarely consider the full range of ways in which all of their activities can create added value. One way to avoid a narrow focus is to draw out not only one's own value chain, but also the value chains of one's customers and suppliers and the linkages between the chains.[46] Such an exercise can highlight ways to reduce buyers' costs, improve buyers' performance, reduce suppliers' costs, or improve suppliers' performance. Some apparel manufacturers, for instance, have found new ways to satisfy department store buyers that have nothing to do with the physical character of the clothes. By shipping clothes on the proper hangers and in certain containers, for example, these manufacturers can greatly reduce the labor and time required to transfer clothes from the department store loading dock to the sales floor.

4. In rapidly changing markets, it is often valuable to pay special attention to leading-edge customers *if* their demands presage the needs of the larger marketplace. Yahoo!, the Internet search engine firm, releases test versions of new services to sophisticated users to shake down software and sense the future needs of the wider market.[47]

5. Underserved customer segments represent a significant opportunity. Circus Circus, the casino operator, built much of its remarkable success (a return on equity exceeding 40% in the early 1990s) on the insight that Las Vegas offered

little to the family-oriented segment of the market. Overserved customers also offer an opportunity, as Southwest Airlines realized.

6. More generally, one of the most potent ways that a firm alters its added value is by adjusting the *scope* of its operations.[48] Broad scope tends to be advantageous when there are significant economies of scale, scope, and learning (including vertical bargaining power based on size), when customers' needs are relatively uniform across market segments, and when it is possible to charge different prices in different segments. Of course, broader isn't always better: there may be diseconomies rather than economies of size, and attempts to serve heterogeneous customers may introduce compromises into a firm's value chain or blur its external or internal message by creating cognitive conflicts in the minds of customers or employees.[49] And even when broader *is* better, there tend to be a variety of ways in which a firm can expand its reach, some of which (such as licensing, franchises, or strategic alliances) fall short of an outright expansion of scope.

In general, a firm should scour its business system for, and eliminate, activities that generate costs without creating commensurate willingness to pay. It should also search for inexpensive ways to generate additional willingness to pay, at least among a segment of customers.

THE WHOLE VERSUS THE PARTS

The analysis described in the previous section focuses on decomposing the firm into parts—that is, discrete activities. In the final step of exploring options, however, the management team must work vigilantly to build a vision of the whole. After all, competitive advantage comes from an *integrated set* of choices about activities. A firm whose choices do not fit together well is unlikely to succeed.

The importance of internal fit can be visualized, once again, in terms of our metaphor of the business landscape. What particularly complicate the search for high ground—or added value—on this landscape are the interactions among choices: Production decisions affect marketing choices, distribution choices need to fit with operations decisions, compensation choices influence a whole range of activities, and so forth. Graphically, the interactions make for a rugged landscape characterized by lots of local peaks, as depicted on the cover of this book.[50] The peaks denote coherent bundles of mutually reinforcing choices.

The ruggedness of the business landscape has several vital implications. First, it suggests that incremental analysis and incremental change are unlikely to lead a firm to a new, fundamentally higher position. Rather, a firm must usually consider changing many of its activities in unison to attain a higher peak. To improve its long-run prospects, a firm may have to step down and tread through a valley. (Consider the wrenching and far-reaching changes required to turn around IBM, for instance.)

Second, the ruggedness implies that more than one internally consistent way to do business often exists within the same industry. Although only a limited number of viable positions are available, more than one high peak usually appears when the interactions among choices are rich. In the retail brokerage business, for instance, both Merrill Lynch and Edward Jones have succeeded historically, but they have done so in very different ways. Merrill Lynch operates large offices in major cities, provides access to a full range of securities, advertises nationally, offers in-house investment vehicles, and serves corporate clients. Edward Jones operates thousands of one-broker offices in rural and suburban areas, handles only conservative securities, markets its services through door-to-door sales calls, produces none of its own investment vehicles, and focuses almost exclusively on individual investors.[51]

The landscape metaphor also reminds us that the creation of competitive advantage involves *choice*. In occupying one peak, a firm forgoes an alternative position. And it highlights the role of competition: It is often more valuable to inhabit one's own, separate peak than to crowd onto a heavily populated summit. Finally, the landscape provides additional perspective on the techniques for industry analyses that were discussed in Chapter 2. It suggests, at least to us, less emphasis on analyzing average industry attractiveness—which might be envisioned as the average height of the landscape above sea level—and more emphasis on understanding the industry features that influence the locations of peaks and troughs and their evolution over time.

SUMMARY

The analysis in this chapter helps systematize part of the older SWOT (strengths-weaknesses-opportunities-threats) paradigm for strategic planning because strengths and weaknesses often vary substantially, even among direct competitors. As a result, within-industry differences in performance tend to be significant, and businesses that aim to be particularly successful typically must position themselves to create competitive advantages within their industries.

Competitive advantage depends on driving a wider wedge between buyers' willingness to pay and costs than one's competitors can. The concept of added value helps integrate considerations of competitive advantage/disadvantage and industry-level conditions into assessments of the likely profitability of individual businesses. A business has added value when the network of customers, suppliers, and complementors in which it operates is better off with it than without it—that is, when the firm offers something that is unique and valuable in the marketplace.

To achieve a competitive advantage or a higher added value than its rivals, a business must do things differently from them on a day-to-day basis. These differences in activities, and their effects on relative cost position and relative willingness to pay, can be analyzed in detail and used to generate and assess options for creating competitive advantage.

In addition to decomposing the business into activities, however, its managers must also craft a vision of an integrated whole. Much power can be derived, in particular, from positive, mutually reinforcing linkages among activities that make the whole more than the sum of its parts.

Finally, we must emphasize that discussions of positioning risk being static instead of dynamic. Some of this risk flows from the terminology itself. It would probably be better to talk about targeting a path for continuous improvement than to discuss settling into a position for all time. Additionally, positioning has a connotation of choosing from a preset, well-specified set of possibilities, whereas coming up with new positions—fundamentally new ways of competing—can have very high payoffs and therefore demands strategic attention. But there is one problem with the basic theory of positioning that is more than semantic: While achieving lower costs or delivering greater benefits than competitors can lead to competitive advantage, can such differences be expected to persist over time, and if so, why? These questions are discussed in the next chapter of this book, on competitive dynamics.

GLOSSARY

added value	market segmentation
choice	mass customization
competitive advantage	opportunity costs
competitive position	resources
cost analysis	rugged landscape
cost drivers	scope
deaveraging	segmentation
differentiation	sensitivity analysis
dual competitive advantage	strategic options
field maps	trade-offs
"focus" option	unrestricted bargaining
"generic" strategies	value
horizontal differentiation	value chain
internal consistency	vertical differentiation
internal fit	willingness to pay

NOTES

1. R. Rumelt. "How Much Does Industry Matter?" *Strategic Management Journal* 1991; 12:167–185. A. M. McGahan and M. E. Porter, "How Much Does Industry Matter, Really?" *Strategic Management Journal* 1997; 18:15–30. A. M. McGahan, "The Influence of Competitive Position on Corporate Performance." Harvard Business School mimeograph, 1997.

2. Anita M. McGahan and Michael E. Porter. "The Emergence and Sustainability of Abnormal Profits," unpublished working paper, Harvard Business School, 1998.

3. Richard Caves and Pankaj Ghemawat, "Identifying Mobility Barriers." *Strategic Management Journal* 1992; 13:1–12. J. W. Rivkin. "Reconcilable Differences: The Relationship Between Industry Conditions and Firm Effects." Harvard Business School mimeograph, 1997. Also see Anita McGahan and Michael Porter. "How Much Does Industry Matter, Really?" *Strategic Management Journal* 1997; 18:15–30.

4. The challenge of creating competitive advantage at a point in time is separated in this book, as in many other treatments, from the problem of *sustaining* advantage over time, even though the two

issues clearly intersect. Sustainability is the major theme of Chapters 4 and 5.

5. See Michael S. Hunt. "Competition in the Major Home Appliance Industry." DBA dissertation, Harvard University, 1972. Two other dissertations at Harvard—Howard H. Newman, "Strategic Groups and the Structure-Performance Relationship: A Study with Respect to the Chemical Process Industries," and Michael E. Porter, "Retailer Power, Manufacturer Strategy and Performance in Consumer Good Industries"—elaborated and tested the notion of strategic groups. A theoretical foundation for strategic groups was provided by Richard E. Caves and Michael E. Porter. "From Entry Barriers to Mobility Barriers." *Quarterly Journal of Economics*, November 1977: 667–675.

6. See, for instance, Kenneth J. Hatten and Dan E. Schendel. "Heterogeneity within an Industry: Firm Conduct in the U.S. Brewing Industry, 1952–71." *Journal of Industrial Economics* 1997; 26:97–113.

7. This conclusion is based on one of Pankaj Ghemawat's experience working at BCG in the late 1970s.

8. Michael E. Porter. *Competitive Advantage* (New York: Free Press, 1985), Chapter 2.

9. For a recent review of activity-based analysis from the perspective of cost accounting, see Robin Cooper and Robert S. Kaplan. "Profit Priorities from Activity-Based Costing." *Harvard Business Review* 1991; 69:130–135.

10. Interestingly, the founders of both Bain and SPA had worked on a BCG study of Texas Instruments that was supposed to have highlighted the problem of shared costs. See Walter Kiechel III. "The Decline of the Experience Curve." *Fortune,* October 5, 1981.

11. Quoted in Walter Kiechel III. "The Decline of the Experience Curve." *Fortune,* October 5, 1981.

12. The term "differentiated" is often misused. When we say that a firm has differentiated itself, we mean that it has boosted the willingness of customers to pay for its output and that it can command a price premium. We do not mean simply that the company is different from its competitors. Similarly, a common error is to say that a company has differentiated itself by charging a lower price than its rivals. A firm's choice of price does not affect how much customers are intrinsically willing to pay for a good—except when price conveys information about product quality.

13. Interview with Joseph Bower, April 25, 1997.

14. Interview with Fred Gluck, February 18, 1997.

15. Michael Porter. *Competitive Strategy* (New York: Free Press, 1980), Ch. 2; William K. Hall. "Survival Strategies in a Hostile Environment." *Harvard Business Review* Sept./Oct., 1980:78–81.

16. Michael E. Porter. *Competitive Advantage* (New York: Free Press, 1985), p. 33.

17. Talk by Arnoldo Hax at Massachusetts Institute of Technology, on April 29, 1997.

18. Michael E. Porter. *Competitive Strategy* (New York: Free Press, 1980), pp. 41–44.

19. Recently, McDonald's has chosen to charge lower prices than its rivals for comparable items. See S. Chandaria, S. Khan, M. O'Flanagan, R. O'Hara, and S. Parikh. "McDonald's: Have the Golden Arches Lost Their Luster?" In: M. E. Porter, ed. *Case Studies in Competition and Competitiveness.* (Harvard Business School, 1997).

20. R. Hallowell. "Dual Competitive Advantage in Labor-Dependent Services: Evidence, Analysis, and Implications." In: D. E. Bowen, T. A. Swartz, and S. W. Brown, eds. *Advances in Services Marketing and Management* (Greenwich: JAI Press, 1997).

21. M. E. Porter. *Competitive Strategy* (New York: Free Press, 1980), Ch. 2; M. E. Porter. "What Is Strategy?" *Harvard Business Review* 1996; 74:61–78.

22. A. M. Brandenburger and B. J. Nalebuff. *Co-opetition* (New York: Doubleday, 1996), pp. 127–130.

23. Cynthia A. Montgomery. "Marks and Spencer, Ltd. (A)," ICCH No. 9-391-089.

24. See, for instance, Pankaj Ghemawat. *Commitment* (New York: Free Press, 1991), Ch. 4. For some empirical studies that seem to support this conclusion, see Lyn Philips, David Chang, and Robert D. Buzzell. "Product Quality, Cost Position and Business Performance: A Test of Some Key Hypotheses." *Journal of Marketing* 1983; 47:26–43; Danny Miller and Peter H. Friesen. "Generic Strategies and Quality: An Empirical Examination with American Data." *Organization Studies* 1986; 7:37–55.

25. A. Christian, P. McDonald, and A. Norris. "Goldman Sachs." In: M. E. Porter, ed. *Case Studies in Competition and Competitiveness* (Harvard Business School, 1997).

26. G. Jacobson. "Enterprise's Unconventional Path." *New York Times,* January 23, 1997.

27. Adam M. Brandenburger and Harborne W. Stuart, Jr. "Value-Based Business Strategy." *Journal of Economics and Management Strategy* 1996; 5:5–24.

28. Adam M. Brandenburger. "Bitter Competition: The Holland Sweetener Company Versus NutraSweet (A)," ICCH No. 9-794-079.

29. This conclusion assumes, of course, that NutraSweet would continue to expand its capacity in line with rapidly growing demand—something that might have appeared quite uncertain to HSC. One limiting feature of added value analysis in its current form is that it doesn't allow for informational complexities of this sort, although it may turn out to be generalizable.

30. In the event, HSC was able, later on, to get paid to stay.

31. Such expedients have variously been referred to as "judo economics" or the "puppy-dog ploy." See Judith Gelman and Steven Salop. "Judo Economics: Capacity Limitation and Coupon Competition." *Bell Journal of Economics* 1983; 14:315–325; Drew Fudenberg and Jean Tirole. "The Fat Cat Effect, the Puppy Dog Ploy and the Lean and Hungry Look." *American Economic Review* 1984; 74:361–368.

32. This section draws heavily on ideas first developed in M. E. Porter. *Competitive Advantage* (New York: Free Press, 1985), especially Chs. 2–4. Also see Pankaj Ghemawat. *Commitment* (New York: Free Press, 1991), Ch. 4.

33. D. Narayandas and V. K. Rangan. "Dell Computer Corporation," Harvard Business School Case 596-058, 1996.

34. N. Siggelkow, "Firms as Systems of Interconnected Choices: The Evolution of Activity Systems." Harvard Business School mimeograph, 1997.

35. M. E. Porter. *Competitive Advantage* (New York: Free Press, 1985), Chs. 2–4; M. E. Porter. "What Is Strategy?" *Harvard Business Review* 1996; 74:61–78.

36. The authors thank Roger Martin of Monitor Company for this example. Details about the companies and other items have been altered substantially to protect proprietary information.

37. See Pankaj Ghemawat. *Commitment: The Dynamic of Strategy* (New York: Free Press, 1991), Ch. 4, for a more extensive list of general guidelines.

38. See M. E. Porter. *Competitive Advantage* (New York: Free Press, 1985), Ch. 3; D. Besanko, D. Dranove, and M. Shanley. *Economics of Strategy* (New York: John Wiley, 1996), Ch. 13.

39. R. E. Caves and P. Ghemawat. "Identifying Mobility Barriers." *Strategic Management Journal* 1992;

13:1–12. Of course, this general pattern may or may not hold up in a particular setting.

40. See M. E. Porter. *Competitive Advantage* (New York: Free Press, 1985), Ch. 4; D. Besanko, D. Dranove, and M. Shanley. *Economics of Strategy* (New York: John Wiley, 1996), Ch. 13.

41. W. J. Salmon and D. Wylie. "Calyx and Corolla." Harvard Business School Case 592-035, 1991.

42. We present "low price" as an attribute that buyers seek. This statement should not be misunderstood as meaning that price determines willingness to pay. Rather, price is included as an attribute in surveys of customer needs so that one can calibrate the willingness of customers to pay a price premium for the other attributes in the survey (such as freshness).

43. See, for instance, P. Kotler. *Marketing Management: Analysis, Planning, Implementation, and Control.* (Englewood Cliffs: Prentice-Hall, 1994).

44. B. J. Pine. *Mass Customization: The New Frontier in Business Competition.* (Boston: Harvard Business School Press, 1993).

45. O. Harari. "The Myths of Market Research." *Small Business Reports* July 1994:48 ff.

46. M. E. Porter. *Competitive Advantage* (New York: Free Press, 1985).

47. M. Iansiti and A. MacCormack. "Developing Products on Internet Time." *Harvard Business Review* 1997; 75:108–117.

48. Scope has a number of dimensions—horizontal, vertical, and geographic—that were discussed in Chapter 2. The discussion here focuses on horizontal and geographic scope. Vertical scope, which raises a different set of issues, is discussed at greater length in Chapter 4, in the context of hold up.

49. M. E. Porter, "What Is Strategy?" *Harvard Business Review,* Vol. 74, No. 6, 1996, pp. 61–78.

50. D. Levinthal. "Adaptation on Rugged Landscapes." *Management Science* 1997; 43:934–950; J. W. Rivkin. "Imitation of Complex Strategies." Harvard Business School mimeograph, 1997. The landscape metaphor is derived from evolutionary biology, especially S. A. Kauffman, *The Origins of Order* (Oxford: Oxford University Press, 1993).

51. R. Teitelbaum. "The Wal-Mart of Wall Street." *Fortune* October 13, 1997;128–130.

CHAPTER 4

Anticipating Competitive and Cooperative Dynamics

> The motive of success is not enough. It produces a short-sighted world which destroys the sources of its own prosperity. The cycles of trade depression which afflict the world warn us that business relations are infected through and through with the disease of short-sighted motives.
>
> —*Alfred North Whitehead*

*C*hapter 3 began with advice to build the better mousetrap. But better mousetraps attract imitators as well as mice. More broadly, in most business situations, players' payoffs depend not only on their own actions, but also on the actions of other players that are pursuing their own purposes. This chapter discusses ways of anticipating how the interactions among interdependent players will evolve over time. It thereby adds a dynamic dimension to the discussion of competitive advantage in Chapter 3.

We begin by considering ways to think through competitive (and cooperative) dynamics when a small number of identifiable players are involved. We then examine evidence about the general unsustainability of competitive advantages and review four evolutionary dynamics that threaten sustainability. The overarching implications for strategies aimed at building and sustaining superior performance are discussed in Chapter 5.

COMPETITION AND COOPERATION AMONG THE FEW

The obvious way of analyzing competitive (and cooperative) dynamics among a few players is to use detailed information about those firms to anticipate their likely actions or reactions and develop strategies to forestall or blunt threatening moves. Two very different theories have been proposed for doing so: game theory and behavioral theory. Behavioral theory (or, at least, behavioral common sense) made an earlier mark on business strategy; practical applications of game theory to business, in contrast, remain so novel as to be the subject of considerable excitement.[1] We will begin by discussing game theory, however, because it helps place behavioral views of interactive decision making in context.

Game Theory[2]

Game theory is the study of interactions among players whose payoffs depend on one another's choices and who take that interdependence into account when trying to maximize their respective payoffs. A general theory of *zero-sum games,* in which one player's gain is exactly equal to the other players' losses (e.g., chess), was supplied more than 50 years ago in John von Neumann and Oskar Morgenstern's pathbreaking book, *The Theory of Games and Economic Behavior.*[3] Most business games, however, are *non-zero-sum games* in the sense that they afford opportunities for both cooperation and competition. Non-zero-sum games have been studied under two different sets of assumptions: as *freewheeling games* with unrestricted bargaining, in which players interact without any external constraints, and as *rule-based games,* in which interactions are governed by specific "rules of engagement."[4] In freewheeling games, which were mentioned in Chapter 3, no good deal goes undone; as a result, a player cannot hope to earn more than its added value. In this chapter, we focus on the uses and limits of rule-based game theory to analyze competitive dynamics among a few players.

Rule-based game theory is being used by a growing number of companies to make decisions about marketing variables, capacity expansion and reduction, entry and entry-deterrence, acquisitions, bidding, and negotiation. The major contribution that the theory makes is that it forces managers to put themselves into the shoes of other players rather than viewing games solely from the perspective of their own businesses. It would be difficult to do justice to rule-based game theory in a book, let alone one chapter.[5] Here we will simply illustrate its uses and limits by considering an actual example derived from a pricing study for a major pharmaceutical company.

The client (henceforth denoted as C) sold a highly profitable product that dominated its category, but was bracing for the introduction of a therapeutic substitute by another major pharmaceutical company. As the late-mover, the entrant (henceforth denoted as E) was expected to launch its product at a very large discount despite its greater therapeutic benefits. It was unclear, however, exactly how low E's launch price would be and whether C should reduce its own price in anticipation or reaction. The cash flows involved were large enough, however, to compel careful consideration of C's options.

The analysis began by specifying four options, involving different levels of discounting, for E's launch price. In addition, it identified four options for C's own (relative) price that were bracketed by the alternatives of holding C's price level constant and of neutralizing E's price advantage. Experts helped gauge the market share implications of each pair of prices. These market shares were then combined with knowledge of C's costs and estimates of E's costs to calculate the net present values (NPVs) of the two products for their respective companies in the "payoff matrix" depicted in Exhibit 4.1. The first entry in each cell gives the estimated payoff for C and the second entry (following the slash) estimates the payoff for E.[6]

E X H I B I T 4.1 ▬▬▬▬▬▬▬▬▬▬▬▬▬▬▬▬▬▬▬

The Pharmaceutical Payoff Matrix (millions of dollars)

Client's (C's) Price	Entrant's (E's) Price			
	Very Low	Low	Moderate	High
No price change	358/190	507/168	585/129	624/116
E has large price advantage	418/163	507/168		
E has small price advantage	454/155	511/138	636/126	
C neutralizes E's advantage	428/50	504/124	585/129	669/128

This schematic became the centerpiece of the pricing study. First, it raised questions about the existing business plan, which assumed that E would launch with a high price and that C would not change its price at all. The modeling revealed that this "base case" was a highly unlikely outcome: If C didn't change its prices at all, E would have a strong incentive to launch its product with a very low price, increasing its NPV by $75 million (65% of the base-case payoff), and reducing C's NPV by $267 million (to 57% of the base-case payoff). Furthermore, if E did launch with a very low price, C's best response was to cut its own price substantially, leaving E with only a small price advantage. This option increased C's NPV by $96 million, to 73% of its base-case payoff. In the event that neither player was able to precommit to a particular strategy, this last outcome (a very low launch price for E and concession of a small price advantage by C) represented the only equilibrium (or stable) point for this game, with unilateral deviations from this point costing more than $10 million per player.

This equilibrium point, however, was highly unattractive to C's managers, who saw it as career-threatening. Instead, they began to explore whether they could change the game by credibly precommitting to a (relative) pricing strategy for their product. A credible precommitment to ceding a large price advantage to E might, given the payoff matrix, persuade E to launch with a low price rather than a very low price (E stood to make an extra $5 million, or 3% more, by doing so) and increase C's payoffs from 73% of the base-case payoff to 81% (a difference of $53 million). And a credible precommitment to neutralizing E's price advantage was even more likely to persuade E not to launch with a very low price: E stood to make an extra $74–$79 million, more than doubling its NPV, by entering with a low to moderate price. In particular, if C committed to neutralize E's price advantage and E entered with a low price, C's payoffs would approximate 81% of the base case; if E entered with a moderate price instead, C's payoffs would increase by $80 million, to 94% of the base-case payoff. Subsequent work centered on figuring out whether this "neutralization" strategy could credibly be implemented.

This example illustrates how modeling business situations as simple, quantifiable games can yield major payoffs. Game theory forced client managers to think about the launch price that would maximize the entrant's profits instead of fixating on the high launch price that they *wanted* to see the entrant adopt.

Game-theoretic analysis is sometimes formalized by drawing up "reaction functions." In the context of the pharmaceutical example, for instance, this step involved identifying the entrant's best pricing response to each possible choice by the client, and vice versa. When reaction functions intersect at just one point, as they did in that case, the intersection represents the unique equilibrium—the unique set of mutually consistent actions—under the assumption that players move simultaneously. In contrast, if one player can move first, as C aspired to do by the end of the study, it can attempt to select its preferred point off the reaction function(s) of its rival(s). This difference underscores the importance of timing and the order of moves in rule-based games.

Reaction functions can offer useful insights into competitors' incentives without necessarily identifying a unique equilibrium point. For example, an increase in price by one competitor is likely to induce its rivals to (1) follow suit if their reaction functions slope upward or (2) cut their prices if their reaction functions slope downward. And even when reaction functions themselves cannot be identified with any degree of precision, role-plays, simulations, and lessons from the academic literature on game theory may—by forcing managers to think explicitly about the incentives and likely moves of competitors—generate valuable insights about ways to shape or adapt to their moves.

Game-theoretic thinking is most helpful when there are only a few players whose actions or reactions really matter for a particular issue. In the pharmaceutical example, expanding the number of players in the financial model would have exploded the number of "cells" to be considered: from 16 cells with two players, to 64 cells with three players, to 256 cells with four players. In fact, there were a total of five players, including the entrant, in the product market that was analyzed, but two were excluded on the grounds that they were marginal players without a discernible impact on market outcomes, and a third was eliminated because its unique product characteristics insulated it from interactions between C and E, and vice versa. The number of players under consideration can also sometimes be reduced by aggregating players with similar economics and objectives.

Several additional factors also influence the benefits from game-theoretic analysis. Identifiable (rather than faceless) players, relatively clear-cut options for them, and good data sources all facilitate the task of mapping actions into payoffs. Players' familiarity with one another and repeated interactions among them increase the likelihood that they will actually reason or grope their way to game-theoretic equilibrium, enhancing its usefulness as a reference point. Attractive structural features—in addition to the presence of a small number of players—expand the scope for game-theoretic analysis, enabling it to generate counterintuitive "cooperative" insights. (The pharmaceutical pricing study would not have been of much avail if competition within the target product market studied could have been counted on to drive prices down to players' costs.) Finally, an organization's embrace of an analytical culture can significantly ease its assimilation of game-theoretic techniques and analysis. In particular, as the pharmaceutical example illustrates, sophisticated financial analysis is usually a complement to, rather than a substitute for, game theory in improving economic outcomes.

Even when these conditions are generally satisfied, simplifications tend to be necessary—as in any model-building exercise—before we can apply game theory to a strategic issue. Common simplifications include reducing the number of players under consideration, fixing the values of particular parameters so as to simplify their effects, suppressing uncertainties, and collapsing the timing structure of the situation, often into a one- or two-stage game representation.[7] These tactics place a premium on looking for robust rather than exact solutions and on conducting sensitivity analyses. Thus, in the pharmaceutical study, caution was called for in assuming that small differences in (estimated) payoffs would definitely lead the entrant to pick one launch price over another. One sensitivity analysis in this case involved accounting for the price-sensitivity of aggregate demand (rather than assuming that it was price-inelastic, as in the basic model), although this choice did not dramatically enhance the attractiveness of the low-price equilibrium.

These procedural guidelines do not, however, address the most common question about game theory: How useful is it in prescribing a course of action if you can't be sure that your competitors will act rationally (that is, follow game-theoretic principles)?[8] One way of finessing this question is to assume that even if competitors fail to maximize their own economic value, they *nevertheless* maximize some well-defined objective function. Thus, the pharmaceutical study dealt with possible "myopia" on the part of the entrant by supplementing analysis based on total NPVs with analyses in which the entrant based its choices on cash flows or total pretax income in the first five years after entry. This approach is a very ad hoc fix, however. For a more general treatment of these issues, we must consider the behavioral approach to analyzing competitive interactions.

Behavioral Theory

To examine behavioral theory, let's reconsider the bitter competition (described in Chapter 3) that broke out when Holland Sweetener Company (HSC) entered the aspartame market, which Nutrasweet had previously monopolized. Rough calculations indicate that the fight between the two reduced the contribution margins in the industry to $150 million per year compared with a potential level in excess of $700 million per year if Nutrasweet had accommodated HSC's relatively small capacity addition. Why, then, did fighting take place?

As in most cases, it *is* possible to rationalize this sequence of events in purely game-theoretic terms.[9] With the exception of true-blue game-theorists, however, few readers are likely to see these events strictly as interactions between two players that sought to maximize their respective profits at each and every point in time. Instead, there is evidence that individuals and firms often irrationally escalate commitment in conflicts because of the "sunk cost" fallacy, attempts to justify past choices, selective perception, hostility, and various other biases and distortions.[10] These biases exemplify the sorts of effects on which behavioralists tend to focus.

The behavioral basis for predicting competitors' actions and reactions was anticipated 40 years ago by Philip Selznick, who observed that "Commitments to ways of acting and responding are built into the organization."[11] This insight, loosely informed by findings in experimental psychology and economics, has inspired a number of templates for predicting competitor behavior. A relatively early example of this sort is provided by Porter's framework for competitor analysis, which comprises four principal diagnostic components: future goals, assumptions, current strategy, and capabilities (see Exhibit 4.2).[12] According to Porter, the first two components, which drive the future behavior of competitors, are less likely to be given their due in practice than the last two, which pertain to what competitors are doing or can do. In addition to roughly 60 factors that supposedly influence these four principal components, Porter enumerates approximately 20 sources of data and 20 options for compiling, cataloging, digesting, and communicating information about competitors, and suggests that an ongoing effort at ana-

E X H I B I T   4.2

A Framework for Competitor Analysis (*Source:* Michael Porter. *Competitive Strategy.* (New York: Free Press, 1980), Chapter 3)

	What Drives the Competitor	**What the Competitor Is Doing and Can Do**
Future Goals At all levels of management and in multiple dimensions	**Competitor's Response Profile** Is the competitor satisfied with its current position? What likely moves or strategy shifts will the competitor make? Where is the competitor vulnerable? What will provoke the greatest and most effective retaliation by the competitor?	**Current Strategy** How the business is currently competing
Assumptions Held about itself and the industry		**Capabilities** Both strengths and weaknesses

lyzing competitors is essential. He also emphasizes the importance of *interpreting* facts about competitors so as to answer questions about their response profiles.

Although checklists such as Porter's are useful, they have a somewhat motley character. They also tend to miss some of the influences on decision making that have been most clearly validated by behavioral researchers.[13] For example, Porter's list does not explicitly mention the irrational escalation of commitment sometimes noted in actual competitive interactions. A somewhat more integrative perspective, and one that forges a tighter connection with behavioral research, is suggested by Selznick's insight that an organization's history has overarching importance in driving its behavior. Historical factors that persistently influence organizational behavior—largely because they are difficult to change in the short run—include the following: the durable resources, capabilities, and relationships that the organization has built up; the people that it employs (particularly top managers); the way in which personnel are organized and the political coalitions that they have formed; the precedents, norms, and beliefs to which they subscribe; and the organization's historical performance dynamics (which affect its reference points as well as the amount of leeway that it has for departing from value-maximizing courses of action).[14] Chapter 5 will elaborate on some ways in which history affects strategy.

In most situations, behavioral analysis is a complement to, rather than a substitute for, game-theoretic analysis. Behavioral analysis tends to focus on organizational predispositions, while game theory focuses on the economic incentives facing organizations.[15] We can therefore ignore behavioral analysis in analyzing competition among the few only when all players are expected to make rational, economic choices; we can discount game-theoretic analysis only when those players are certain to succumb to noneconomic predispositions. Otherwise, the debate about rationality versus irrationality is simply a diversion: Managers should keep both economic and noneconomic influences on competitors' behavior in view. As a corollary, the kinds of competitor intelligence systems employed in behavioral analysis should also be used to generate the information about competitors' revenues and cost structures that is essential for game-theoretic analysis.

Finally, it is worth emphasizing that game-theoretic and behavioral analyses are subject to the same sorts of limitations. Both require large amounts of data to be effective. Both tend to lose their power when competitors are faceless. And, most critically, both become unwieldy when they must account for more than a few players. The next section of this chapter provides a broader, evolutionary perspective on competitive and cooperative dynamics.

EVOLUTIONARY DYNAMICS

Game theory and behavioral theory both represent relatively "micro" ways of thinking about the interdependence of the players in a market—that is, they involve detailed analyses of the individual players. A third, more "macro" way of thinking about interdependence is in terms of the evolutionary dynamics that tend to buffet businesses over time. The attraction of the biological process of evolution in studying strategy stems from the fact that fundamental concepts like scarcity, competition, and specialization play similar roles in both spheres of inquiry.[16]

How do competitive advantages evolve over time in the world of business? Consider some data analyzed by Ghemawat (1991), concerning the margins (return on investment, or ROI) reported over a 10-year period by 692 business units in the PIMS database.[17] Splitting this sample into two equally sized groups based on initial ROI revealed that the top group's ROI in year 1 was 39% and the bottom group's ROI was 3%. The businesses in the top group, therefore, generally started out with competitive advantages, and those in the bottom group began with competitive disadvantages. If businesses were kept in the groups in which they started out, what changes might you predict to the 36-point spread between the group averages by year 10?

Managers confronted with this question tend to guess that the initial ROI spread between the two groups shrank by one-third to one-half over the 10-year period (with significant dispersion around this central tendency). Exhibit 4.3 indicates that the correct answer is that the gap diminished by greater than nine-tenths. By implication, managers understand the idea of regression toward the mean, or mediocrity, but fall short in assessing the scope and speed of its operation.

Many others have developed similar data illustrating how quickly above-average performance collapses toward the averages. A study by Fruhan (1997) of large companies with an average return on equity (ROE) of more than 25%

EXHIBIT 4.3

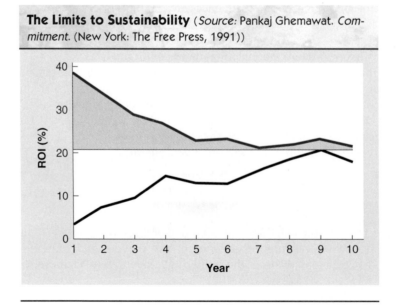

The Limits to Sustainability (*Source:* Pankaj Ghemawat. *Commitment.* (New York: The Free Press, 1991))

between 1976 and 1982 found that the median ROE of this top group was 21% higher than the average for the Standard and Poor's 400 for this early period, but only 2% higher in the 1989–1993 period.[18] A study by Foster and others at McKinsey & Company, after defining excellence in terms of ROE plus sales growth, came to similar conclusions about its impermanence.[19]

Some of the quick regression of above-average returns back toward the averages presumably reflects value-maximizing choices: A business earning a 39% ROI (the average in year 1 for the top group studied by Ghemawat) is unlikely to insist that all new investments deliver such a high rate of return, and likely to be unwise if it did. However, most of this regression toward the mean seems to be unwanted and even unanticipated. Perhaps the most obvious evolutionary analogy is with the "Red Queen" effect, named after the character in Lewis Carroll's *Through the Looking Glass,* who explains to Alice that "Here, you see, it takes all the running you can do to keep in the same place." The business version of the Red Queen effect is the idea that, as organizations struggle to adapt to competitive pressures, their fitness levels improve, raising the baseline against which competitive advantage has to be measured. In landscape terms, this dynamic might be interpreted as a tendency for old mountain peaks to subside over time.

It will be useful, however, to be more concrete about the causal processes that threaten the sustainability of peak performance. The rest of this chapter unbundles threats to sustainability into two dynamics—imitation and substitution—that threaten businesses' added value and two others—holdup and slack—that threaten their owners' ability to appropriate that added value for themselves (see Exhibit 4.4).

E X H I B I T 4.4

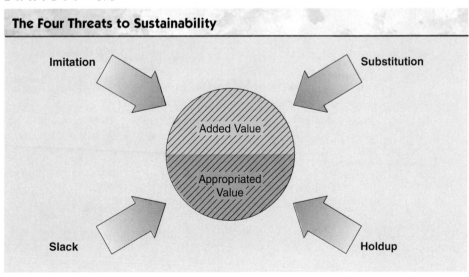

The Four Threats to Sustainability

Imitation

Substitution

Added Value

Appropriated Value

Slack

Holdup

THREATS TO ADDED VALUE

Imitation and substitution both threaten the sustainability of a business's added value. *Imitation* is most frequently invoked in biology in the context of the population pressures within a species that fuel the "struggle for existence."[20] In terms of business strategy, imitation can be envisioned as the diffusion of successful business models—defined in terms of resources deployed and/or activities performed—across the population of firms. Imitation in this sense diminishes the extent to which the originator of a successful business model would be missed if it simply disappeared (a heuristic for added value, as noted in Chapter 3).

Substitution, as an evolutionary dynamic, is a less direct threat to added value than imitation, although no less important. In biological terms, substitution can be interpreted as competition between (rather than within) species. In terms of business strategy, it can be envisioned as the threat of being displaced by a different business model.

Imitation

Imitation is, according to the cross-industry evidence, pervasive. Attempts by one player to increase its capacity, for example, often trigger additions by competitors intent on preserving their capacity shares. Attempts to build one's customer base tend to prompt competitors to defend or develop their own. Furthermore, attempts at product differentiation based on R&D (as opposed to marketing strategies) are vulnerable on several counts: Aggregate data indicate that competitors secure detailed information on the bulk of new products within one year of their development, patent-based strategies usually fail to deter imitation, and imitation tends to cost one-third less than innovation and to be a third quicker to market. Process innovations do not seem to be significantly less imitable than product innovations.[21]

Imitation is not always bad. Imitation can sometimes lend credibility to a new product (e.g., when network externalities or second-sourcing is an issue). Also, the imitation of certain types of marketing moves such as loyalty schemes and meet-the-competition clauses doesn't necessarily undermine their effectiveness.[22] When imitation is broad enough to threaten to transform a supposedly unique business model into something quite generic, however, it typically does hurt the added value of the business(es) that originally developed that model. In landscape terms, imitation that depresses added value can be interpreted as the subsidence of a peak as an increasing number of firms clamber toward or crowd onto it.

Part of the reason imitation can be so hazardous to companies' financial health relates to how far it can proceed. Although classical economics indicates that imitation will be curtailed when imitators' profits drop to zero, informational and motivational considerations suggest that it may proceed even further. One relevant strand of microeconomic research concerns "information cascades," in which players inferring information from the actions of other participants rationally decide to ignore their own information and act alike—even in situations where they might do better, on average, by acting differently.[23] Another strand of work shows that managers may, to preserve or gain reputation when markets are imperfectly informed about their abilities, either "hide in the herd," so as to avoid being evaluable, or "ride the herd," so as to signal quality.[24] It is possible to think of noneconomic reasons for "herding" as well, such as envy or norms.

HSC's entry into the market for aspartame provides one example of imitation that apparently proved unprofitable for the imitator while significantly depressing the innovator's profitability. Another instance in which imitation seems to have overshot the zero-profit condition involves the case of prime-time network television in the United States. The three established networks (ABC, CBS, and NBC) have historically competed with one another principally on the basis of their programming. Casual observation suggests that their programming decisions have tended to look alike along a number of measures, ranging from when they announce their schedules for the upcoming year (May), to when they introduce new programs (September), to the topical focus of those new programs. Thus *The X-Files* (introduced by Fox), was a highly successful 1990s program focused on extraterrestrials and the supernatural—but not the only one. Imitators included *Profiler, Dark Skies, The Burning Zone, The Visitor, Prey,* and *The Psi Factor,* a number of which quickly flopped.

Some of the similarity in the networks' programming decisions over time may be due to shifts in viewer preferences: Westerns, for example, accounted for at least 10% of the network prime-time schedule in the 1960s, but their combined share dropped to 3% in the early 1970s. A broader analysis by Robert Kennedy suggests, however, that shifts in demand do not provide the whole story behind the topical bunching of the programs introduced by the three traditional networks.[25] Starting with a data set that classified all prime-time television programming by the networks into 15 categories, Kennedy tracked each network's introductions in each category (867 in total) over a 28-year period (1961 to 1989). He found that when one network emphasized a particular category of program in its new introductions, rivals tended to emphasize the same category—even after accounting for changes in the total Nielsen ratings points per category and the average rating per show in that category. In addition, Kennedy showed that programs introduced in trendy categories (defined as the top third of new programming categories) experienced, on average, significantly lower ratings and shorter lives than programs introduced in nontrendy categories (defined as the bottom third). Exhibit 4.5 summarizes the average differences.

As a postscript, it is worth noting that imitative behavior along these and other dimensions did more than just directly depress the profitability of the three traditional networks. It also left room for Fox to become the first successful entrant into the industry since the 1950s by employing—particularly initially—a very different programming strategy.[26] Fox's emergence as a full-fledged network in the 1990s put further pressure on the added values of the networks by affecting the advertising dollars that they could charge and the terms on which they could procure programming (e.g., rights to broadcast professional football games).

Trends and Success in the Programming of New Television Series (*Source:* Data from Robert E. Kennedy. "Strategy Fads and Competitive Convergence: An Empirical Test for Herd Behavior in Prime Time Television Programming." Unpublished working paper, Harvard Business School, January 1998)

Averages	Year 1 Ratings	Year 3 Ratings	Years Broadcast	% Surviving 3 Years
Trendy introductions	15.3	16.4	1.8	21%
Nontrendy introductions	16.3	20.4	2.3	27%

Reflecting that reality, author Ken Auletta titled his best-selling book on the networks *Three Blind Mice*.[27]

Despite these dire examples, imitation does not always pose an inescapable threat to the sustainability of a competitive advantage: It sometimes can be, and is, deterred. Economists have used game-theoretic models to test the efficacy of various barriers to imitation in the presence of alert competition by considering possibly asymmetric outcomes and asking whether the laggards can cost-effectively close the gap with the leaders.[28] Strategists have, in addition, flagged mechanisms that might make imitation intrinsically infeasible rather than simply cost-ineffective. The list of barriers to imitation that follows covers both sorts of mechanisms, although it does not purport to be either mutually exclusive or completely exhaustive. In fact, imitation is least threatening when multiple barriers to imitation reinforce each other.

Economies of Scale and Scope   The most obvious barrier to imitation is that supplied by scale economies, namely, the advantages of being large in a particular market or segment. If scale is advantageous, a business may potentially deter imitation by committing itself to being so large that would-be imitators are held back by the fear that if they matched its scale, supply might exceed demand by enough to make them rue the effort. Such scale economies can work on a global, national, regional, or even local level, and their effects need not be confined to manufacturing. A good example of local scale economies in a service business is provided by Carmike, a highly successful operator of movie theaters, which focuses on small towns neglected by other competitors. Most of these towns cannot support two cinemas, so once Carmike makes an investment in a multiplex theater to service such a town, it gains an imitation-proof local monopoly.

Scope economies are a second familiar form of size economies: They derive from the advantages of being large in interrelated markets or segments. They can work just like scale economies in deterring imitation. For example, if a company can share resources or activities across markets or segments while ensuring that its costs remain largely fixed, it may be able to stake out a large, profitable position for itself. In addition, even in the absence of such opportunities for sharing, bundling complementary goods or services can elevate barriers to imitation. Of course, exploiting scope economies in any of these ways requires extensive coordination across markets or segments.

Learning/Private Information   Learning, especially if interpreted in terms of the experience curve, can be envisioned as a third form of size economies, albeit one that relates to the advantages of being large in a particular business over time rather than at one point in time. But instead of revisiting size-based deterrence here, we can consider a different kind of impediment to imitation that underlies learning effects: superior information or know-how. To the extent that superior information can be kept private—that is, to the extent that it is costly for would-be imitators to tap into it—imitation will be inhibited. Although a policy of nondisclosure can sometimes ensure privacy, many other channels of potential informational leakage exist, including suppliers, customers, spinoffs, reverse-engineering, and even patent documents. As a result, privacy of information is most achievable when information is tacit rather than specifiable (i.e., doesn't lend itself to blueprinting), and when it is collectively held by the organization, rather than consisting of something that one or two parties can carry out the door. We will expand on these themes when we discuss the development of superior capabilities in Chapter 5.

Contracts and Relationships   It may sometimes be possible to enter into contracts or establish relationships with buyers, suppliers, or complementors on better terms than those available to late movers. When such arrangements are enforceable, competitors may desist from imitation on the grounds that even if this approach "succeeded," it would leave them at too much of an absolute disadvantage—independent of differences in size or information—to be worthwhile. Enforceability may derive either from third-party enforcement or from self-enforcement. Examples of third-party enforcement include property rights and other formally specified contracts that are enforceable in court. Strategists have, in this context, placed particular emphasis on the control of physically unique resources (e.g., owning or having a long-term lease on the best retail location in town). Examples of self-enforcement include relationships that have not been formalized to the same extent but are nevertheless expected to be sustained by reputations, switching costs, risk aversion, or inertia. We will probe enforceability in more detail later on in this chapter, when we look at the threat of holdup.

Network Externalities   As barriers to imitation, network externalities embody elements of scale, complementarity, learning effects, and relationships—all of the barriers previously discussed. They are nevertheless worth mentioning separately because of the amount of attention they have aroused in the context of the information economy.[29] Network externalities exist when the attractions to buyers, suppliers, or complementors of joining a network increase with its size. In such cases, even very small size advantages tend to snowball over time, amplifying the advantage of the firm that controls the largest network (if such proprietary control is possible, in contrast to open standards, for example).

For a striking example, consider how Nintendo managed to drive up willingness to pay while reducing its costs in the video game business.[30] Nintendo's large installed base of hardware attracted the best software houses to develop games for it. The (expected) availability of numerous hit games increased customers' willingness to pay high prices for Nintendo's software and their tendency to buy many of its machines, especially since Nintendo periodically upgraded its technology. This allowed Nintendo and its hardware suppliers to move down the experience curve, reducing hardware costs and prices over time and further increasing the network's advantage. Nintendo cemented its control over this network by installing a security chip that prevented non-Nintendo games from being played on Nintendo machines, and by imposing a range of contractual restrictions on its developers and retailers.

Threats of Retaliation   There are a number of reasons, including the asymmetries cited above, why a business with an advantage may be able to threaten would-be imitators with massive retaliation. The certitude of retaliation may, in turn, deter the imitation of a strategy even when its present profitability is very high. Talk of retaliation is, however, cheap. To be credible, it must be backed up by both the ability and the willingness to retaliate. The ability to retaliate is facilitated by the successful creation of a competitive advantage that allows a business to do better for itself than with a strategy of accommodation while threatening an interloper with losses. The ability to retaliate is also enhanced by the maintenance of "buffer" stocks, such as liquidity, excess capacity, small positions in competitors' other businesses that can be used to disrupt them, fighting brands, and even product upgrades that remain warehoused until competitors threaten to imitate existing product offerings.

Being willing to retaliate, and credibly communicating as much to would-be-imitators, is simplest when retaliatory moves are directly profitable to the advantaged business—a possibility that is often enhanced by targeting retaliation or picking avenues of retaliation that are relatively cost-effective. Thus an early mover with a large market share might retaliate against interlopers by escalating R&D or advertising, both of which often have important fixed cost components, rather than by cutting price, which typically has a more variable effect and therefore ends up costing large players more in absolute terms. The credibility of retaliation can be enhanced in a variety of other ways as well: by writing contracts that make retaliation more attractive than retreat, otherwise binding oneself (e.g., the approach of "burning one's bridges" or brinkmanship), cultivating a reputation for retaliating against imitators, and even signaling (although such signals usually need to be supplemented by something more irreversible if they are to be credible).

Time Lags   Even if all of the barriers to imitation described earlier are lacking, imitation usually requires a minimum time lag. Implicit in such time lags is the idea that crash programs can be costly: The principal reason is that attempts to use time ever more intensively may lead to diminishing returns. When such time lags exist, they obviously defer the impact of imitation. The prospect of such lags can also deter imitation altogether, especially when the innovator has set up a virtuous cycle (à la Nintendo) or is continuously upgrading its position (as discussed later in this chapter).

Guesstimates of the average duration of time lags help underscore their importance.[31] As a rule of thumb, marketing variables—particularly those related to communications—are the only ones that can be changed significantly in less than one year; even so, the customer bases that they are supposed to influence tend to move much more slowly. It takes two to three years to build the average manufacturing plant. Some evidence suggests that building a new distribution system or altering an existing one may take even longer. The mean lag in returns from expenditures on research and development tends to be on the order of four to six years. The lags in implementing major changes in human resource practices, building company reputations, and restructuring corporate portfolios may stretch out over the better part of a decade or even longer!

Strategic Complexity   Another set of barriers to imitation encompasses the notion of complexity. Behaviorally oriented strategists have argued that the very complexity of a strategy may, in a world characterized by low to variable rationality, impede its imitation.[32] Others have sought to pin down the sources of complexity and have come up with several different answers. One proposal cites "causal ambiguity"—the idea that intrinsic ambiguity may shroud the causal connections between actions and results or, more prosaically, that a successful firm may itself be uncertain about what really makes it tick.[33] Another proposal emphasizes "social complexity," which may place certain resources—corporate culture is the favorite example—beyond the ability of firms to systematically manage and influence.[34]

A third proposal focuses on "fit" as the relevant source of strategic complexity. This proposal differs substantially from the previous two because, instead of positing complexity, it derives complexity—in a strict algorithmic sense—from the interconnectedness of the choices that firms make.[35] The landscape metaphor suggests some helpful imagery in this regard: As the interconnectedness of choices increases, the landscape facing a firm becomes progressively more rugged in a way that explodes the complexity of mapping it completely—or even of "just" identifying the highest peak. Chapter 5 examines how salient fit should be on the strategist's agenda.

Upgrading   Last, but hardly least, among barriers to imitation is continuous upgrading of the organization's own added value. This strategy involves driving a wider wedge between customers' willingness to pay and suppliers' opportunity costs over time, and it often requires investment to achieve this end. Upgrading is supposed to transform a business into a moving target in a way that compounds the difficulties or delays for potential imitators. One way to account for the need to upgrade is to track the rate at which an industry's real prices, adjusted for changes in quality, change over time. If an industry's average prices decrease by more than a threshold rate (2% to 8% per year, according to Jeffrey Williams), it is a "fast-cycle" environment in which continuous upgrading is particularly important.[36] Other spurs to upgrading include tactics such as imagining, like topflight runners, that a business has phantom competitors at its heels every step of the way.[37] The bias toward action built into upgrading also reminds us that barriers to imitation *can* be constructed: They are not just nice things that happen to lucky firms.

Substitution

Added value may be threatened by substitution as well as by imitation. Substitution is often seen as the threat that one product will displace another. It should actually be envisioned more broadly—that is, as the threat that new business models will displace old ones. Consequently, substitution can pose an even deadlier threat to sustainability than imitation, as emphasized more than half-a-century ago by the economist Joseph Schumpeter:[38]

> It is still competition within a rigid pattern of invariant conditions, methods of production and forms of industrial organization in particular, that practically monopolizes attention. But in capitalist reality as distinct from its textbook pictures, it is not that kind of competition which counts but the competition from the new commodity, the new technology, the new type of organization . . . competition which commands a decisive cost or quality advantage and which strikes not at the margins of the profits and the outputs of the existing firms but at their foundations and their very lives. This kind of competition is much more effective than the other as a bombardment is in comparison with forcing a door.

In landscape imagery, substitution can be depicted as an earthquake—or a landscape shift, at least—that pushes up new peaks and pulls down existing ones. It is, in that sense, both less direct and more difficult to manage than the threat of imitation by direct competitors trying to clamber up the same peak. Today, it seems to command much more attention among business strategists than it did in Schumpeter's era: Substitution has prompted the publication of numerous books about value migration, disruptive technologies and, more broadly, shifting bases of competition.

For a vivid—and still unfolding—example of a substitution threat, consider online stock trading.[39] Online execution of stock trades in the United States increased from negligible levels five years ago to 17% of total retail volume in 1997, and is forecast to account for nearly 30% of trading volume in 1998 and more than 50% within three years. There are already about 5 million active online trading accounts, and they generate more trades on average than do conventional

EXHIBIT **4.6**

The Economics of Brokerage Business Models, Early 1996
(*Source:* Rajiv Lal. "E-Trade Securities, Inc." Stanford University Graduate School of Business, Case No. M-286, 1996)

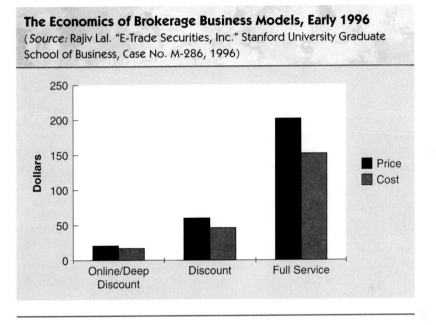

accounts. Although one can cite a host of reasons to explain the popularity of cybertrading—such as the availability of timely information, convenience, one-on-one marketing, and even the allure of online investment communities such as Motley Fool—by far the most important reason for going online seems to be its lower prices, which are underpinned by lower employee, occupancy, and data processing/communications costs. Exhibit 4.6 provides some estimates for early 1996, when E*Trade, the pioneering online broker, was charging $15–20 per trade. Since then, online prices have decreased further, to less than $10 per trade in some instances.

Recognizing the cost differences between online and offline business models, a number of conventional players have moved aggressively into online trading. Conventional discount brokers, from whom online trading has so far drawn most of its customers, have led the way. Particularly noteworthy is Charles Schwab, which pioneered discount brokerage in the mid-1970s, the use of independent financial planners as complementors in the mid-1980s, and easy switching into and out of mutual funds in the early 1990s. As of 1998, Schwab had set up a slew of transactional and informational sites on the Web in an effort to migrate as many of its customers as possible onto the Internet. Its "mid-market" positioning relied on its reputation, information about its existing customers, creative product and service development, and responsiveness to lock in business despite its premium prices: The company's basic eSchwab online trading service was priced at $29.95, compared with E*Trade's price of $14.95 and prices as low as $8 for other online brokers. In addition, only a minority of Schwab's online customers actually used eSchwab: The majority simply received a 20% discount for trading online. Despite some doubts about the sustainability of its price structure, Schwab's strategy seemed to be working as of mid-1998: It had 1.8 million active online accounts and a 29% share of the total online trading volume, compared with 11% for the next largest player (E*Trade), and it executed more than $2 billion in trades per week.

No conventional full-service brokers have moved online nearly as aggressively as Schwab or other discount brokers. In fact, the two national full-service firms, Merrill Lynch and Prudential Securities, that *had* announced plans to offer online trading repeatedly postponed the launch of those services through 1997 and the first half of 1998. In addition, reports indicated that they would not offer any discounts online off their full-service rates—an unlikely recipe for retaining existing customers eyeing online trading, let alone acquiring new ones. Interestingly, major commercial banks, such as Bank of America and Wells Fargo, have made a more aggressive foray into online brokerage, albeit as an adjunct to the automation of their traditional banking transactions with the public.

The example of online stock trading illustrates the most obvious trigger of substitution: drastic, cross-cutting technological change (of which the Internet is just one particularly current example). But substitution, as a threat to added value, encompasses much more than just technological change. Other "supply-side" triggers of substitution include changes in input prices or availability and deregulation (or, more broadly, changes in governmental policies). For example, the electricity sector in Latin America is being reshaped by the increased availability of cheap natural gas and the push throughout most of the region to privatize electricity generation and distribution, rather than by technological change per se. On the "demand side," triggers of substitution include changes in customer preferences, previously unmet needs and changes in the customer mix. Thus, while online retailers may use the Internet to target leading-edge customers, some observers think that rather different business models will be needed to cater to the emergent mass market.

The experience of online stock trading also suggests the difficulties that incumbents often face in responding to substitution threats. Consider online trading from the perspective of a leading full-service broker such as Merrill Lynch. From this vantage point, online trading is still a very small niche in revenue (rather than volume) terms: Online activity accounted for slightly more than 4% of total (retail) brokerage commissions in 1997, with its share projected to reach between 6% and 7% in 1998. Second, the immediate profit prospects in online trading appear to be poor. In addition to an environment characterized by a steep drop in prices, 75 competitors were already online by mid-1998, up from 30 in mid-1997. Some observers estimated that, in battling for market share, these companies might spend as much as $500 million on advertising in the next 12 months (compared with $600 million in total revenues in 1997). Third, online trading currently seems to underserve the needs of many of the full-service firms' customers. Fourth, moving aggressively into online trading would effectively require cannibalization of broker and branch networks consisting, in Merrill

Lynch's case, of 15,000 financial consultants and 700 branches. Fifth, at least some traditional brokerage firms lack the expertise necessary to invest efficiently and effectively in Net-based businesses. Finally, considerable ambiguity persists regarding which business model, if any, will win out in online brokerage. Specialized online trading is just one of the possibilities: other contenders include commercial banks, coalitions that are trying to create and control mechanisms for online billing and payment, critical issues developers of personal financial management software, and portals for online access.

This discussion of why full-service brokers might have difficulty responding to online substitution threats suggests that we can construct a generic list of barriers to response that incumbents have to be wary of and that attackers can exploit. Substitution threats typically start out in small, initially unprofitable niches. At first, the new entrants tend to underserve the needs of existing customers, upon whom incumbents may focus. The threats often inspire mixed motives on the part of incumbents because they bring up fears of self-cannibalization. Countering the threats may require skills or expertise that incumbents do not have and cannot effectively acquire. And early on, substitution threats are often surrounded by ambiguity as to which of several possible business models will win out.[40]

Note that this short list of barriers to effective response does *not* include the corporate sins that are popularly cited as opening the door to substitution threats: sloth, arrogance, myopia, bureaucracy, politics, and the like. The possibility of such maladaptive behavior adds to the difficulty of responding to substitution threats. The good news, however, from the perspective of incumbents, is that substitution threats *can* sometimes be deterred, deflected, or turned into opportunities. Schwab's ability to seize the lead (so far) in online brokerage is a good example. Managers must, however, first recognize the barriers to response cited above if they are to respond successfully to substitution threats. Recognizing the range of possible responses is a second helpful step. Although responses to substitution threats are often framed in terms of the fight-or-switch dichotomy, it is usually better to begin by considering a broader array of alternatives.

Not Responding   The best response to substitution threats is sometimes no response at all. Not all substitution threats are equally threatening or successful. Sometimes, a careful, forward-looking assessment of a substitution threat may suggest that it does not pose a significant threat to a firm's added value. Consider, for instance, Ernie, the "retail consulting" service recently launched by the accounting firm of Ernst & Young; it allows clients to e-mail questions and receive responses within 48 hours for the payment of what is, by the standards of traditional consulting, a tiny retainer. It is not clear that top management consulting firms, such as McKinsey & Company and the Boston Consulting Group, should respond to this initiative at this time. Of course, the danger in not responding is that the barriers to response cited earlier may inappropriately bias assessments toward inaction.

Fighting   Fighting is a more commonly recognized response to substitution threats. For example, Intel fought off the threat that reduced instruction set computing (RISC) technology posed to its complex instruction set computing (CISC) technology by making massive investments to improve the performance of its CISC-based microprocessors. In this way, Intel raised both customers' willingness to pay for its technology and the cost hurdles confronting the sponsors of the substitute technology. One key danger associated with fighting, however, is that a substitute at an early stage in its development may have more long-run improvement potential than a mature business model.[41]

Switching   Switching is another commonly recognized response to substitution threats. Successful switching is, especially in fast-moving environments, like changing horses in mid-stream: There is sometimes no alternative but the maneuver *is* subject to spills. An example of successful switching through the mid-1990s is provided by Quantum. Unlike many of its competitors in the computer disk drive industry, this company managed to make the transition from 8-inch drives to 5.25-inch drives to 3.5-inch drives to 2.5-inch drives.[42] Of course, Quantum's task was probably made easier by the fact that the successive substitutes were more of a degree than of a kind in its industry—that is, not as wrenching as, say, the threat to the conventional brokerage business model from online substitutes.

Recombining   Switching carries the connotation of adopting a business model that is, in some sense, already "out there." In many cases, however, recombining elements of one's existing model with some of the new possibilities implicit in substitution threats seems to represent a more successful response to substitution threats than the wholesale switching of business models. Recombination possibilities tremendously expand the range of possible responses to substitution threats. Schwab's strategy in online brokerage provides a good example of this type of response: Instead of switching to the deep-discount models offered by the initial entrants into online brokerage, it tried to create a hybrid business model that melds some of its existing strengths with online technology. The danger with such recombination strategies, however, is that one may end up with the equivalent of a camel rather than a race horse—that is, a business model that is very oddly put together.

Straddling   Straddling involves continuing to operate traditional business models as well as adopting new ones. Some traditional retailers that have gone online provide examples of this response. Straddling can be a valuable short-run expedient to preserve an organization's options even when it is not a viable long-run strategy. Straddles can also be distinguished in terms of whether they are balanced between the old and the new business models or not (e.g., offer just a toehold in the new business model). These ideas about straddling also call attention to the timing and magnitude of responses to substitution threats as additional variables that can be used to further expand the range of possible responses. Perhaps the biggest dangers with straddling relate to excessive commitment to an old business model that is no longer viable, or an unwillingness to make tough choices.

Harvesting   Harvesting one's business is not the stuff about which inspirational books are written, but it can nevertheless be the correct response to a substitution threat when none of the other strategies makes sense. Harvesting may, for instance, be the appropriate response for some conventional brokers that lack the scale, resources, or technological expertise to do much about the threat from online trading. Harvesting once again raises interesting issues of timing. Like all of the responses to substitution threats considered in this section, it carries its own dangers. Clayton Christensen's study of technological substitution threats, for example, found that while harvesting seems to be the most common pattern of response by incumbent firms, it is often accidental, at least in the early stages of the process.[43]

To conclude this section, there are no fool-proof, all-purpose responses to substitution threats. If such a response existed, substitution would be less of the killer that it often seems to be. Nevertheless, recognition of both the typical barriers to effective response and the broad array of possible responses should help a player address such indirect threats to the sustainability of its added value.

THREATS TO THE APPROPRIABILITY OF ADDED VALUE

Even if an organization can protect its added value from the threats of imitation and substitution, the ability of its owners to appropriate that added value cannot be taken for granted. There are two systematic threats to value appropriation over time: holdup and slack. Holdup threatens to divert value to buyers, suppliers, complementors, or other players in the firm's network. Slack, in contrast, threatens to dissipate value over time.

Holdup

Holdup stems from cospecialization, which is a special case of a broader dynamic that biologists refer to as coevolution. Flowers and the insects that pollinate them and feed on their nectar provide an obvious example. Similar mutualism can be beneficial, even essential for success, in the business world, but it can potentially create a problem as well: As players cospecialize, their added values begin to overlap, making it impossible for all participants to appropriate the full amount. Each can therefore be said to face the threat of being held up by the others.[44]

The clearest conceptual example of holdup is provided by the case of bilateral monopoly, which involves just one seller and one buyer. Such a setting is characterized by complete cospecialization: The added value of each player is equal to the total value that the two create by transacting with one another. Yet both cannot count on appropriating the whole amount. Instead, the value appropriated by one player is exactly equal to the size of the wedge that holdup drives between the other player's added value and appropriated value.

The changing parts relationship between auto makers and their suppliers offers a vivid example of the threat of holdup as well as different ways of responding to it. By the mid-1970s, automaker–supplier relationships in the United States seemed to have stabilized around a model in which the Big Three—General Motors (GM), Ford, and Chrysler—generally manufactured at least some of their requirements of any basic component in-house (up to 100% in the case of "critical" items such as engines, transmissions, and axles), while outsourcing the rest to a number of suppliers. Their relationships with these outside suppliers, celebrated at the time, were frankly adversarial.[45] GM and Ford, in particular, fragmented their supplier base by using multiple suppliers and by encouraging entry. The Big Three narrowed suppliers' ability to differentiate themselves by maintaining large in-house R&D staffs, forcing innovators to license or otherwise reveal their technology, breaking down systems into parts, and making every part into a commodity through comprehensive specifications. Contracts rarely ran for more than one year, and they would not be renewed if the auto maker found another qualified supplier offering even a fractionally lower price. Other mechanisms that were employed to force prices down included using inspection teams to estimate suppliers' costs, letting small, low-overhead suppliers make low bids that could be used in negotiations with other suppliers, linking price concessions on a particular part sourced from a large supplier to continued purchases of other parts, and even starting rumors about potential competition.

Then the Japanese auto makers entered the fray. While many factors were responsible for Japanese auto makers' stunning success in the U.S. automobile market, the contribution of their supplier relationships, as documented by Jeffrey Dyer and other researchers, became increasingly apparent through the 1980s.[46] Despite less vertical integration, Japanese auto makers worked with as a few as one-tenth of the number of suppliers employed by U.S. auto makers. They maintained long-term relationships with their suppliers, shared detailed technical and cost information with them, and involved them in both product development and production. Japanese suppliers, in turn, invested in assets specific to the auto makers that they served (see Exhibit 4.7). To consider just one dimension, the average distance between Toyota's plants and its suppliers' plants was less than 60 miles, compared with 400 to 500 miles for plants owned by U.S. auto makers and their suppliers. In fact, the bulk of Toyota's production network in Japan could fit between GM's two closest plants, both in Michigan. This policy of geographic proximity carried over to Toyota's and its suppliers' investments in production in the United States, most of which were located in Kentucky.

The Japanese model led to clear-cut reductions in inventories, which accounted for 11.3% of sales for Japanese auto makers and their suppliers combined, compared with 19.5% for U.S. auto makers and their suppliers. On comparable cars, Japanese auto makers enjoyed total cost advantages of 10%–20%. At the same time, 30% fewer problems were reported for Japanese cars, and new-model cycle times were 40% shorter. Unsurprisingly, average profitability, as measured in terms of pretax return on assets, was significantly higher in Japan through the early 1990s—9.3% for Japanese auto makers and 5.5% for their suppliers, compared with 3.7% and 4.6%, respectively, for their U.S. counterparts.

E X H I B I T   4.7 ▰▰▰▰▰▰▰▰▰▰▰▰▰▰▰▰▰▰▰▰▰▰▰▰▰▰▰

Asset-Specificity in the Automobile Industry (*Source:* Jeffrey H. Dyer. "Does Governance Matter?" *Organization Science,* 1996; 7(6))

Measures of Asset-Specificity	United States/United States			Japan/Japan	
	Arm's-length (42%)*	Partner (10%)*	Division (48%)*	Arm's-length (35%)*	Partner (38%)*
Distance between manufacturing plants (miles)	589	413	276	125	41
Capital that is not readily redeployable (%)	15	18	31	13	31
"Person-days" of face-to-face contact divided by sales to auto maker (index)	7.7	9.0	7.9	9.9	10.6
Supplier's sales to auto maker divided by supplier's total sales	34	34	94	19	60

*Share of part production.

These advantages have probably narrowed in recent years as U.S. auto makers, and particularly Chrysler, have moved to varying degrees to imitate the Japanese approach to supplier relations. And even the continuing differences do not necessarily indicate that more cospecialization is always better. When the level of trust or task interdependence is low and (perhaps) when the level of environmental turbulence is high, less cospecialization may be more appropriate. Nevertheless, in at least one salient industry, U.S. manufacturers appeared to lose ground partly because they took a very competitive approach to supplier relationships (seeking to maximize their bargaining power at the expense of the suppliers), whereas their Japanese competitors took a more cooperative tack (cospecializing so as to grow the overall pie). This example echoes one of the major dicta introduced in Chapter 2: Strategists must think about relationships both cooperatively and competitively.

The auto supply example also illustrates a range of approaches for dealing with holdup that includes trying to obviate the problem as well as approaching it competitively or cooperatively.

Contracting   One of the first remedies for holdup that U.S. auto makers tried was long-term contracting.[47] As demand for cars shifted from open, largely wooden bodies toward closed metal bodies after World War I, large investments in metal stamping machines became important. To encourage such investments, GM signed a 10-year contract with Fisher Body in 1919, whereby it agreed to buy substantially all of its closed bodies from Fisher at operating costs plus a percentage markup. During the next few years, however, demand for autos shifted toward closed bodies and grew more rapidly than expected. GM came to think that it was being held up by Fisher, because substantial increases in throughput had significantly reduced Fisher's capital costs per body to an extent unanticipated in the original contract. For its part, Fisher refused to locate its body plants next to GM's assembly plants (despite GM's insistence that proximity was necessary for efficiency) for fear of being held up by GM.

The broader implication of this dispute is that totally comprehensive contracts enforceable at zero cost—the sorts of contracts that could theoretically eliminate holdup—are generally impractical. Reasons include bounded rationality, uncertainty about the future, and asymmetric information.[48] Interestingly, Japanese auto makers and suppliers relied on informal safeguards rather than the formal contracts emphasized by their U.S. counterparts to prevent holdup problems from getting out of hand.

Integrating   To solve the problems that resulted from its 10-year contract with Fisher Body, GM entered into negotiations to purchase Fisher in 1924, culminating in the two companies' merger in 1926. Integrating vertically in this fashion (or horizontally to cope with complementors) is an obvious way of tackling a holdup problem.[49] The modern experience of U.S. auto makers, which became much more integrated than their Japanese rival, suggests, however, that vertical integration is no panacea. Vertical integration may breed inflexibility, bureaucracy, incentive problems (e.g., sticking with the internal supplier through thick and thin), and slack, as discussed in the next section. It may also expose firms to greater holdup problems along dimensions other than the ones on which they originally focused. For instance, the size and clout of the United Automobile Workers' (UAW) union in the United States might have been smaller today and less of an impediment to the restructuring of supplier relationships had less vertical integration taken place in the industry's past. Finally, the superior performance of Japanese auto maker–supplier relationships suggests that decisions to integrate may need to be subject to a stiffer test than "Can we do this task internally more efficiently than via market mechanisms?" Interorganizational relationships may sometimes offer a better basis for dealing with holdup-related issues than either market transactions or the managerial hierarchies induced by integration, as discussed below.

Building Bargaining Power   Another obvious way of dealing with holdup-related issues is to create competition on the other side of the divide while retaining uniqueness (and added value) on one's own side. Building asymmetric dependence or bargaining power in this way improves one's own "best alternative to a negotiated agreement" (BATNA) with a particular supplier, buyer, or complementor while reducing the partner's BATNA.[50] As noted earlier, U.S. auto makers traditionally relied on a host of tactics to create competition: maintaining large internal R&D and production efforts, fragmenting the outside suppliers (which were used anyway), and limiting the ability of any one supplier to differentiate itself from the rest of the pack. Although Japanese auto makers didn't push the creation of competition on the supply side that far, they did not exactly ignore the issue. Instead, Japanese auto makers often adopted dual-sourcing from "outside" suppliers even when it limited the achievement of economies of scale. If large performance differences did develop between two outside suppliers of a component or subassembly, Japanese auto makers typically worked with the weaker supplier so as to keep it in the game.

Bargaining Hard　In addition to building purchasing power to deal with holdup related issues, U.S. auto makers traditionally sought to leverage that power by adopting a tough negotiating posture. Manifestations of this tactic included short-term contracts (often not renewed), a focus on prices in contracting or recontracting decisions, a willingness to use linkage or sequencing to force larger multipart suppliers to fall into line, posturing, bluffing, and restrictions as picayune as ruling out lunches with suppliers' representatives. Despite an increase in U.S. auto makers' formal commitment to closer relationships with their suppliers by the 1990s, they continued to bargain hard, leaving suppliers with the perception that they still would not be treated fairly in situations where they did not have formal contractual protection. As a result, the emergent pattern of supplier relationships in the U.S. auto industry might be described as closer but still adversarial.

Reducing Asset-Specificity　Reducing asset-specificity is sometimes an independent lever that can be pulled to reduce the extent of the holdup problem. In other cases, it accompanies (or is a response to) attempts to build up one's bargaining power or to bargain hard. Although the evidence indicates that this "solution" was pushed too far in U.S. auto supply, the reduction of asset-specificity is not always a losing proposition. In the metal can industry, for example, Crown Cork & Seal attempted to mitigate buyer bargaining power by not locating its plants where they would effectively be dedicated to just one buyer. This approach presumably worked better in the metal can industry because the level of task interdependence between can manufacturers and their buyers was lower than that between auto parts suppliers and auto makers.

Building Relationships　Unlike the three previously discussed methods for dealing with holdup problems—all of which emphasized the minimization of dependence on the other side, even if it shrank the total size of the pie—a fourth, very different approach is evident in Japanese auto makers' relationships with their parts suppliers (and particularly with affiliated, rather than independent, companies). Although Japanese suppliers were dependent on Japanese auto makers, dependence ran both ways: Most parts supplied by partners were "black boxes," with the auto maker providing only general specifications and the supplier preparing all of the detailed specifications and blueprints. This made it difficult to change suppliers. Both sides effectively invested in expanding the total profit stream that would be available to them only *if* they continued to work together. The broader conceptual point is that if partners make substantial investments that are specific to each other and each are accorded a large enough share of the joint gains from cooperation, such interorganizational relationships may prove self-enforcing. That is, opportunistic behavior may be held in check by the fear that the larger profit stream available from cooperation might then disappear.[51]

Developing Trust   The stability of cooperative relationships is enhanced when trust is high. Trust depends, in part, on the cultural and historical context. The Japanese business environment, for example, has often been contrasted with the U.S. business environment as placing more emphasis on social institutions (norms, expectations, and so on) than on legal institutions to check opportunistic behavior. Japanese auto makers may have benefited from this general social ambience in setting up cooperative relationships. Nevertheless, they also took proactive steps to build up trust by swapping stock with or acquiring minority interests in their partner companies, transferring employees to and hosting "guest engineers" from their suppliers, sharing information, and cultivating a reputation for fairness rather than transaction-by-transaction maximization of their own profitability. Chrysler's success in enhancing supplier trust within its own, very different cultural and historical context—through steps such as investing in communication and coordination, recognizing past performance as well as suppliers' needs to make a fair profit, soliciting feedback and sharing the savings, shifting toward longer-term contracts, and creating the expectation of business beyond the life of the contract if suppliers performed—suggests that cooperative solutions to the holdup problem are not merely an "only in Japan" story.

Finally, note that the broader context in which a business operates can create another, very different type of holdup threat, one involving unilateral expropriation (i.e., effective revocation of property rights) rather than mutual cospecialization. Although issues of expropriation are most frequently raised in regard to the governments of developing countries, the same issues sometimes crop up in more developed contexts. For instance, the attorneys-general of several dozen states in the United States are currently trying to renege on contingency fees that they agreed to pay private lawyers to orchestrate their lawsuits against the tobacco industry, because the prospects of unexpectedly large settlements have pushed the lawyers' prospective payoffs to levels that are deemed "socially unacceptable." At the federal level, similar concerns may be motivating the current antitrust investigations of Microsoft and Intel, in particular. Although the origins of such nonmarket threats of holdup differ from those of the market-based threats on which most of this subsection has focused, some of the same remedies (with the obvious exception of vertical integration) can be employed to mitigate them.

To summarize, holdup is a systematic threat to the appropriability of added value that is largely based on cospecialization. A range of options exist for dealing with holdup threats; these approaches vary, among other ways, in terms of the extent to which they emphasize competition as opposed to cooperation. A historical bias in strategic thinking toward taking the competitive approach (i.e., maximizing bargaining power in situations where holdup is an issue) should be balanced with the recognition of opportunities for cooperation (i.e., the possibility of growing the pie so as to make each participant in the transaction/relationship better off).

Slack

Slack is an internal threat to appropriation of added value, and one for which no direct biological analogue exists. Slack can be defined as the extent to which the value appropriated by an organization falls short of the amount potentially available to them. In dynamic terms, slack can be thought of as persistent suboptimization by an organization that dissipates appropriable added value instead of passing it on to the owners, or even reduces its added value over time. The ability to withstand large amounts of slack is linked to past economic success and the current existence of potentially appropriable added value. An organization without much in the way of either could not persistently dissipate value and still survive.

Although the conceptual definition of slack is reasonably clear, its measurement can prove difficult. This difficulty springs from several sources. Some "slack" (e.g., a plush headquarters) may be essential to attracting customers (e.g., in businesses such as investment banking and consulting). Some may represent an irreducible requirement for innovation (i.e., for experimentation with new strategies and innovative projects that might not be allowed in a more resource-constrained environment). Some may reflect nonmonetary compensation to employees as a substitute for paying them more. Even more broadly, some "slack" may be required to sustain cooperative relationships with workers or suppliers. Some apparent "slack" may, therefore, be of considerable value.

Despite these difficulties, researchers have made several attempts to measure the extent and implications of slack. Detailed benchmarking of individual activities or processes across companies, particularly across direct competitors, have revealed large differences in productivity levels. Studies that attempt to organize individual activities into production functions and measure how far short individual establishments or firms fall from the fitted "productivity frontier" corroborate the existence of significant amounts of slack. Estimates of the fraction of revenues dissipated, on average, in this fashion range from 10% to 40% for U.S. manufacturing, although such measures yield very unstable estimates when applied across countries.[52] Finally, some evidence is starting to emerge that slack can foster innovation, up to a point.[53]

The creation of "slack" sufficient to pursue innovation, marketing campaigns and other potentially valuable initiatives is a central challenge for many companies, particularly relatively unsuccessful ones. In companies that have successfully sustained their added values over time, however, managers have to spend more time worrying about too much slack than about too little. In plainer language, rich diets tend to lead to a hardening of organizational arteries. For a dramatic illustration of how much slack can result from past success, consider the case of General Motors (GM).

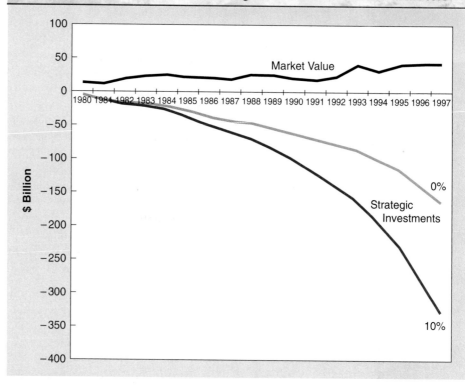

Market Value versus Cumulated Strategic Investments at General Motors

General Motors' financial performance, as measured in terms of returns to shareholders, has been abysmal since the 1980s (see Exhibit 4.8). The market value of the company's stock was $13 billion in 1980 and increased to $42 billion by the end of 1997. Over the same timeframe, however, GM's strategic investments—net capital expenditures plus R&D—added up to $167 billion if simply summed up and $332 billion in terms of their present value in 1997 if compounded at an annual rate of 10%. Even if one assumes that, in the absence of these strategic expenditures, GM's market value would quickly have collapsed to zero and that the company would have been unable to pay stockholders any dividends during 1980–1997, one is still left with the presumption that GM destroyed more than $100 billion of value over this period (and perhaps even more than $200 billion, if one assumes a 10% discount rate).[54] Put another way, the benefit-to-cost ratio of GM's strategic investments between 1980 and 1997 was significantly less than one-half, and perhaps as little as one-third. H. Ross Perot, briefly a director of General Motors, pointed out that GM could have bought Toyota and Honda in the mid-1980s for half of what it spent on itself.

We can explain GM's remarkably poor performance in a number of different ways. Its cars were considered very "boxy," and it failed to respond effectively to the surge in sales of light trucks. It maintained an infrastructure designed to serve 35% of the U.S. market, even though its market share had declined to slightly more than 30%. It had engaged in an extensive automation program that proved remarkably costly and, by many measures, hopelessly ineffective. The company continued to receive poorer marks for its relationships with its parts suppliers than both Ford and Chrysler. Its relationships with the United Auto Workers were arguably worse as well (due, in part, to a history of particularly extensive vertical integration), as indicated by a costly but inconclusive strike in summer 1998. Only in the aftermath of that strike did GM move to spin off much of its parts division and consolidate operations in North America and internationally. The extent to which some of these recently announced changes will be effected remains highly uncertain.

One does not have to dissect the value destruction at GM into these components to point out that value destruction on this scale would not be possible unless GM had accumulated a stupendous potential for slack in prior years. GM was, after all, the largest industrial enterprise in the world—and still is, if measured in terms of revenues. It was able to destroy much more value than its total market value at the beginning of the 1980s presumably because expectations of high, ongoing levels of slack were built into its market valuation.

GM's ongoing struggles with slack two decades after Japanese competition shook up the U.S. auto industry suggest that slack is often sustained by powerful inertial forces. Nevertheless, organization theory does suggest some (partial) remedies for sustained slack that will briefly be mentioned here.[55]

Gathering Information   The difficulty of measuring slack increases, rather than decreases, the importance of gathering information about its extent. Benchmarking against other organizations, particularly direct competitors, is particularly useful in identifying slack. Directly investigating the effects of changes in processes or behavior—an old idea, inherent in time-and-motion studies, that was recently revived as reengineering—provides another way to generate information about opportunities for improvement. Simply gathering more information, however, is unlikely to stamp out all undesired slack because of what Oliver Williamson has referred to as "impacted information": a condition in which one party to a transaction or relationship is much better informed than the other party, which cannot become equally well informed except at great cost, because he or she cannot rely on the first party to be fully candid.[56]

Monitoring Behavior   A second approach to dealing with slack, and one often complementary to the information-gathering option, is to increase the amount of resources devoted to monitoring behavior. Here the goal is to catch inappropriate behavior before it occurs or to decrease its attractiveness by increasing the probability of detection, backstopped by penalties (or by rewards for good behavior). One standard example is making workers punch time clocks and docking their pay if they arrive late or quit early. Note, however, that monitoring is likely to provide only limited benefits when a wide range of discretionary, legitimate choices exist. Is, for instance, a software developer sitting beside a babbling brook with eyes closed slacking off or having an epiphany that will turn out to be commercially valuable?

Offering Performance Incentives   Even when monitoring behavior may be infeasible or uneconomical, it may be possible to reward good behavior indirectly by rewarding good performance. Such an approach works best when an individual's (or group's) behavior is tightly connected to the performance outcomes that are actually observed. This condition is often violated, however, when behavior must be coordinated across individuals or groups in the interests of achieving "internal fit" or when performance can be measured only in highly aggregated terms. Even if we can discount both these problems (e.g., in assessing the performance of top managers), we still lack a good sense of the "appropriate" amount of incentive-intensity. Michael Jensen and Kevin Murphy found, for example, that on average, top U.S. executives receive no more than $3.25 for each $1,000 of shareholder value created.[57] This ratio strikes some people as absurdly low; others regard the resulting pay packages as creating a climate of greed rather than a culture that promotes the effective pursuit of organizational goals.

Shaping Norms   A fourth approach to dealing with slack involves supplementing (or partially replacing) economic rewards and punishments with appeals to norms, values, a sense of mission, and so forth. Underlying this approach is the humanistic idea that people within organizations are sentient beings, motivated by more than just "sticks" or "carrots." Of course, moral suasion is unlikely to be totally effective either. Given the heated debate between economists and other social scientists about the relative efficacy of economic and "intrinsic" motivation, probably the only safe conclusion is that a manager intent on reducing slack can do at least as well by recognizing both types of levers as opposed to fixating on only one of them.

Bonding Resources   Bonding resources is another (economic) approach to containing slack. It is derived from Michael Jensen's theory of free cash flow, defined as "cash flow in excess of that required to fund all projects that have positive net present values when discounted at the relevant cost of capital."[58] According to Jensen, managers are imperfectly policed by shareholders, have incentives to grow the resources under their control, and are particularly able to take such steps when free cash flow is large—leading to what shareholders regard as investments in negative-return activities or pure waste. One obvious remedy, tried by many companies in the second half of the 1980s (but not by General Motors), is to pile up debt so as to reduce free cash flow (by creating contractual obligations to pay fixed interest expenses). Although such attempts have worked in some instances, they have failed in others because the companies became overloaded with debt (i.e., ended up with negative free cash flow).

Changing Governance   Bonding resources is just one of several ways of forcing changes in the top-level control structure of a firm in the hopes of provoking an effective organization-wide response. Other top-down changes intended to deal with slack or, more broadly, the challenges of organizational change, include creating small but well-informed and powerful boards of directors, restricting the abilities of CEOs and other insiders to dominate those boards, requiring board members and top managers to own substantial amounts of a firm's equity (in relation to their personal wealth), encouraging (other) large, active investors, and unwinding cross-subsidies.[59] Some changes of this sort took place at GM in the early 1990s, when a board led by a chairman brought in from outside the company (John Smale, the former CEO of Procter & Gamble) voted to fire GM's then-CEO. GM has yet to turn itself around, however.

Mobilizing for Change   Forcing change at the top may often be necessary to reverse slack-related problems, but it is rarely sufficient by itself. Research in the field of change management suggests that successful organizational change involves the creation of a strong sense of dissatisfaction with the status quo, a powerful vision of what can be accomplished by changing, and a process for change that often involves changing people and organizational structure.[60] Although an in-depth discussion of the process of organizational change lies beyond the scope of this book, we will revisit some of the challenges of change in Chapter 5.

In summary, slack is an internal rather than external threat to the appropriability of added value. That need not imply, however, that slack is easier to control than the other threats to sustainability discussed in this chapter. The scope for slack is highest in companies that have enjoyed, or are enjoying, considerable economic success and is amplified by the difficulties of gathering information, offering high-powered incentives, or otherwise directing the organization toward value-creation instead of value-dissipation.

SUMMARY

The analysis in this chapter has provided a dynamic dimension to Chapter 3's discussion of competitive advantage and added value by discussing ways of anticipating how the interactions of interdependent players will unfold over time. One broad approach is best suited to situations in which there is a small number of identifiable players. In such situations, game theory can help predict players' actions on the basis of their economic incentives, and behavioral theory on the basis of their organizational predispositions. Game theory and behavioral theory are, in this respect, clearly complementary.

A second broad approach is better suited to situations in which players are more numerous or faceless. In such situations, four evolutionary dynamics that threaten the sustainability of actual or targeted advantages should be considered. Two dynamics—imitation and substitution—threaten businesses' added value and two others—holdup and slack—threaten their owners' ability to appropriate that added value for themselves. These evolutionary dynamics are, of course, only general tendencies, not absolute economic laws. Some firms manage to achieve sustainability for significant periods of time despite all of the threats that they face. Still, given the evidence on general unsustainability, understanding these threats should help managers actively anticipate and prepare for changes in the landscapes on which they operate.

A third contribution of this chapter has been to discuss not only threats to sustainability, but also ways of countering those threats (see Exhibit 4.9). Understanding the full range of possible responses increases the likelihood that managers will, in fact, be able to respond successfully to the threats that they face. Having said that, however, it must be granted that the discussion in this chapter has focused on

E X H I B I T 4.9

Responding to Threats to Sustainability

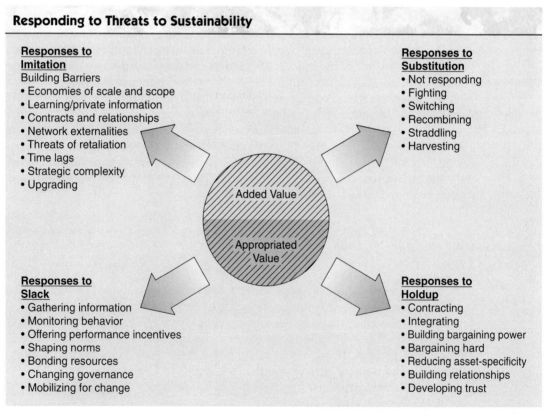

Responses to Imitation
Building Barriers
• Economies of scale and scope
• Learning/private information
• Contracts and relationships
• Network externalities
• Threats of retaliation
• Time lags
• Strategic complexity
• Upgrading

Responses to Substitution
• Not responding
• Fighting
• Switching
• Recombining
• Straddling
• Harvesting

Added Value

Appropriated Value

Responses to Slack
• Gathering information
• Monitoring behavior
• Offering performance incentives
• Shaping norms
• Bonding resources
• Changing governance
• Mobilizing for change

Responses to Holdup
• Contracting
• Integrating
• Building bargaining power
• Bargaining hard
• Reducing asset-specificity
• Building relationships
• Developing trust

the threats one-by-one. In the next chapter, we look at overarching implications of the threats to value—static and dynamic—that we have identified for strategies that aim to build and sustain superior performance.

GLOSSARY

appropriability
barriers to imitation
BATNA
behavioral theory
benchmarking
bilateral monopoly
causal ambiguity
commitments
competitor analysis
complexity
cospecialization
equilibrium
expropriation
fit
free cash flow
freewheeling games
game theory
holdup
imitation
impacted information
incentive-intensity

interorganizational relationships
learning
moral suasion
non-zero-sum games
payoff matrix
privacy of information
productivity frontier
rationality versus irrationality
reaction functions
Red Queen effect
response to substitution
retaliation
rule-based games
scale economies
scope economies
self-enforcement
slack
social complexity
substitution
third-party enforcement
zero-sum games

NOTES

1. This lag seems somewhat paradoxical because economists specializing in industrial organization (IO) turned their attention to game theory in the late 1970s after undertaking—and understanding some of the limitations of—hundreds of empirical studies of the link between industry structure and profitability that helped underpin the "five forces" framework for industry analysis. See Pankaj Ghemawat, *Games Businesses Play: Cases and Models* (Cambridge, MA: MIT Press, 1997), pp. 2–11 for a discussion.

2. This subsection has benefited greatly from discussions with Hugh Courtney and Patrick Viguerie, co-leaders of McKinsey and Company's game theory practice.

3. John von Neumann and Oskar Morgenstern, *The Theory of Games and Economic Behavior* (Princeton: Princeton University Press, 1944).

4. This terminology is based on Adam M. Brandenburger and Barry J. Nalebuff, "The Right Game: Use Game Theory to Shape Strategy," *Harvard Business Review* July–August 1995:57–71. The academic literature on game theory tends to draw a roughly parallel distinction between *cooperative* game theory, which is a theory of combinations, and *noncooperative* game theory, which is a theory of moves.

5. Actually, there is no book-length treatment that quite fits the bill. Brandenburger and Nalebuff's *Co-opetition* (New York: Currency Doubleday, 1996) is written for senior managers but focuses on free-

wheeling game theory. Ghemawat's *Games Businesses Play: Cases and Models* (Cambridge, MA: MIT Press, 1997) does focus on rule-based game theory but is primarily concerned with tracing its uses and limits for academic research in business strategy. The most widely used chapter-length treatment of the importance of looking forward and reasoning back in rule-based games—so as to figure out which of today's actions will lead you to where you want to end up—is probably Avinash Dixit and Barry Nalebuff's "Anticipating Your Rival's Response," *Thinking Strategically* (New York: W. W. Norton & Company, Inc., 1991), pp. 31–55.

6. Three of the cells in the payoff matrix were ruled out as being arithmetically infeasible. In the remaining cells, the payoffs for C were all multiplied by one scale factor and those for E by another so as to preserve client confidentiality. Both the scale factors were significantly less than 1, which should underscore the amount of money at stake. In the last column, payoffs were higher in the bottom cell because it assumed price increases in excess of inflation, unlike the top cell.

7. Two-stage game representations are particularly useful when short-run interactions (e.g., on prices) are used to pin down the outcomes of long-run competition to make investments (e.g., in capacities).

8. The other common question about game theory—how to adapt it to the uncertainties of the real world—lies beyond the scope of this section, although see Ghemawat's *Games Businesses Play: Cases and Models* (Cambridge, MA: MIT Press, 1997) pp. 224–232. Chapter 5 discusses uncertainty and strategy in more general terms.

9. Specifically, Nutrasweet's willingness to slash prices in the relatively small European and Canadian markets, which HSC entered first, can readily be interpreted as an attempt by Nutrasweet to signal its toughness so as to deter entry by HSC into the much larger U.S. market. The subsequent outbreak of hostilities in the United States can be explained, a bit less obviously, in terms of the "fog of war." For an elaboration of the latter idea in the context of another war between duopolists, see A. Brandenburger and P. Ghemawat. "Entry and Deterrence in British Satellite Broadcasting." In P. Ghemawat. *Games Businesses Play: Cases and Models* (Cambridge, MA: MIT Press, 1997), pp. 177–204.

10. Consult, for instance, M. H. Bazerman, and M. A. Neale, *Negotiating Rationally* (New York: Free Press, 1992), Chapter 2, and J. Z. Rubin, D. G. Pruitt, and S. H. Kim, *Social Conflict: Escalation, Stalemate, and Settlement* (New York: Random House, 1994), Chapter 7.

11. P. Selznick. *Leadership in Administration* (Evanston, IL: Row, Peterson, 1957), p. 47.

12. M. E. Porter. *Competitive Strategy* (New York: Free Press, 1980), Chapter 3.

13. Some of the most interesting research of this sort was conducted by Amos Tversky, Daniel Kahneman, and associates; see D. Kahneman, P. Slovic, and A. Tversky, eds. *Judgment under Uncertainty: Heuristics and Biases* (Cambridge: Cambridge University Press, 1992). A recent essay that explicitly tries to summarize some of the implications of this research for anticipating competitors' actions and reactions is R. J. Meyer and D. Banks. "Behavioral Theory and Naïve Strategic Reasoning." In G. S. Day and D. J. Reibstein, eds., *Dynamic Competitive Strategy* (New York: John Wiley, 1997).

14. An interesting organizational perspective on historical sources of inertial momentum is provided by Michael T. Hannan and John Freeman. "Structural Inertia and Organizational Change." *American Sociological Review* April 1984:149–164.

15. This line is admittedly blurred by precommitments—for example, to resources and capabilities—that affect the organization's economic payoffs from doing one thing as opposed to another. Such economic precommitments should, in principle, be folded into the game-theoretic analysis of incentives.

16. J. Hirshleifer. "Economics from a Biological Viewpoint," *Journal of Law and Economics* 1977; 20:1–52. Of course, there are differences as well—particularly the deliberate variation of business strategies that has no obvious counterpart in biology.

17. Pankaj Ghemawat. *Commitment: The Dynamic of Strategy.* (New York: Free Press, 1991), pp. 81–83.

18. William E. Fruhan, Jr. "Stock Price Valuator." Mimeograph, Harvard Business School, 1997.

19. Richard Foster. "The Impermanence of Excellence." In: "Commitment: An Interview with Pankaj Ghemawat." *McKinsey Quarterly* 1992; 3:130.

20. This line of thinking actually originated in economics: Charles Darwin was heavily influenced by Thomas Malthus in this regard.

21. The evidence on imitation is discussed in more detail in Pankaj Ghemawat. "Sustainable Advantage." *Harvard Business Review* (September–October 1986). It also contains specific citations.

22. Adam Brandenburger and Barry Nalebuff. *Co-opetition* (New York: Currency Doubleday, 1996), Chapters 5 and 6.

23. See Sushil Bikhchandani, David Hirshleifer, and Ivo Welch, "Learning from the Behavior of Others: Conformity, Fads, and Informational Cascades,"

Journal of Economic Perspectives (forthcoming) for a general discussion of information cascades, and Henry Cao and David Hirshleifer, "Word of Mouth Learning and Informational Cascades," unpublished working paper, University of Michigan (1997), for a demonstration of the possibility of suboptimal results.

24. See, for instance, Abhijit Bannerjee. "A Simple Model of Herd Behavior." *Quarterly Journal of Economics* 1992:797–818.

25. Robert E. Kennedy. "Strategy Fads and Competitive Convergence: An Empirical Test for Herd Behavior in Prime-Time Television Programming." Unpublished working paper, Harvard Business School (January 1998).

26. Pankaj Ghemawat, Jacquelyn Edmonds, and Scott Garell. "Fox Broadcasting Company." ICCH No. 387-096.

27. Ken Auletta. *Three Blind Mice: How the TV Networks Lost Their Way* (New York: Vintage Books, 1992).

28. Alert competition is assumed because virtually any imaginable asymmetry can be rationalized as the result of inert or stupid competition.

29. W. Brian Arthur. "Increasing Returns and the New World of Business." *Harvard Business Review* July–August 1996:100–109.

30. A. M. Brandenburger. "Power Play (A): Nintendo in 8-Bit Video Games." ICCH No. 9-795-102.

31. Citations for most of these sources can be found in Chapter 5, P. Ghemawat. *Commitment: The Dynamic of Strategy* (New York: Free Press, 1991). See also Richard Hall. "The Strategic Analysis of Intangible Resources." *Strategic Management Journal* 1992; 13:135–144.

32. Paul J. H. Schoemaker. "Strategy, Complexity and Economic Rent." *Management Science* October 1990:1178–1192.

33. Steven A. Lippman and Richard P. Rumelt. "Uncertain Imitability: An Analysis of Interfirm Differences in Efficiency under Competition." *Bell Journal of Economics* Autumn 1982:418–438.

34. Jay B. Barney. "Firm Resources and Sustained Competitive Advantage." *Journal of Management* March 1991:107–111.

35. Jan W. Rivkin. "Imitation of Complex Strategies." Harvard Business School mimeograph, 1997.

36. Jeffrey R. Williams. "How Sustainable Is Your Competitive Advantage?" *California Management Review* Spring 1992:29–51.

37. Peter T. Johnson. "Why I Race against Phantom Competitors." *Harvard Business Review* September–October 1988:106–112.

38. Joseph A. Schumpeter. *Capitalism, Socialism, and Democracy* (New York: Harper, 1942), p. 84. Also

see I. Dierickx and K. Cool. "Asset Stock Accumulation and Sustainability of Competitive Advantage." *Management Science* Vol. 35, No. 12 (December 1989): 1504–1514.

39. This example is mostly based on general information available on the Internet.

40. For a discussion of some of these barriers to response in the context of technological threats, see Clayton M. Christensen. *The Innovator's Dilemma.* (Boston: Harvard Business School Press, 1997).

41. Richard J. Foster. *Innovation: The Attacker's Advantage.* (New York: Summit Books, 1996).

42. Clayton M. Christensen. *The Innovator's Dilemma.* (Boston: Harvard Business School Press, 1997).

43. Christensen, op cit.

44. For the pioneering discussion of holdup, see Oliver E. Williamson. *Markets and Hierarchies.* (New York: Free Press, 1975).

45. See Michael E. Porter. "Note on Supplying the Automobile Industry (Condensed)." ICCH No. 386-176.

46. The principal references employed for this example are Jeffrey H. Dyer and William G. Ouchi, "Japanese-Style Partnerships: Giving Companies a Competitive Edge," *Sloan Management Review* Fall 1993:51–63; Jeffrey H. Dyer, "Specialized Supplier Networks as a Source of Competitive Advantage: Evidence from the Auto Industry," *Strategic Management Journal* 1996; 17:271–291; Jeffrey H. Dyer, "Does Governance Matter? Keiretsu Alliances and Asset Specificity as Sources of Japanese Competitive Advantage," *Organization Science* 1996; 7:649–666; and Jeffrey H. Dyer, "How Chrysler Created an American Keiretsu," *Harvard Business Review* July–August 1996:42–56. Dyer himself bases some of his performance comparisons on data assembled by other researchers.

47. The historical example that follows is based on B. Klein, R. G. Crawford and A. A. Alchian. "Vertical Integration, Appropriable Rents, and the Competitive Contracting Process." *Journal of Law and Economics* 1978; 21:297–326.

48. See Oliver Williamson *Markets and Hierarchies.* (New York: Free Press, 1975).

49. Integration may generate other benefits as well: tying up access to a resource input or a market, improving or protecting information, enhancing coordination, improving the ability to price-discriminate, avoiding taxes (in countries where sales rather than value-added taxes are used), and so on.

50. See R. Fisher, W. Ury, and B. Patton. *Getting to Yes: Negotiating Agreement without Giving in* (New York: Penguin, 1991).

51. For a general discussion of how interorganizational relationships can lead in this fashion to sustained competitive advantage, see Jeffrey H. Dyer and Harbir Singh. "The Relational View: Cooperative Strategy and Sources of Interorganizational Competitive Advantage" forthcoming in the *Academy of Management Review.*

52. Compare Richard E. Caves and David Barton, *Efficiency in U.S. Manufacturing Industries* (Cambridge, MA: MIT Press, 1990), with Richard E. Caves, *Industrial Efficiency in Six Nations* (Cambridge, MA: MIT Press, 1992).

53. Nitin Nohria and Ranjay Gulati, "Is Slack Good or Bad for Innovation?" *Academy of Management Journal* October 1996; 39:1245–1264.

54. For more details on this methodology and an application to General Motors between 1980 and 1990, see Michael C. Jensen. "The Modern Industrial Revolution, Exit, and the Failure of Internal Control Systems." *Journal of Finance* 1993; 48:831–880.

55. For a more extended discussion of some of the ideas touched on here, see Paul Milgrom and John Roberts. *Economics, Organization and Management.* (Englewood Cliffs, NJ: Prentice-Hall, 1992), Chapter 6.

56. Oliver E. Williamson, op. cit., p. 14.

57. Michael C. Jensen and Kevin J. Murphy. "Performance Pay and Top-Management Incentives." *Journal of Political Economy* 1990; 98:225–264.

58. Michael C. Jensen. "Agency Costs of Free Cash Flow, Corporate Finance, and Takeovers." *American Economic Review* 1986; 76:323–329.

59. Michael C. Jensen. "The Modern Industrial Revolution, Exit, and the Failure of Internal Control Systems." *Journal of Finance* 1993; 48:831–880.

60. For a managerial discussion, see John P. Kotter. "Leading Change: Why Transformation Efforts Fail." *Harvard Business Review* March–April 1995:59–67.

5

Building and Sustaining Success

Pankaj Ghemawat and Gary Pisano

> If the actions are dynamic, if top management is able to alternately let chaos reign and then rein in chaos, such a dialectic can be very productive.
>
> —*Andrew S. Grove*

*T*he last two chapters suggested tests of value that a strategy must meet if it is to be successful. First, a strategy must fit together internally in a way that generates added value for the organization as a whole in the environment in which it operates. Second, it must fit with the external environment in a way that immunizes it, at least to some extent, against threats to its sustainability. Such value-based tests improve on the analytical rigor and dynamism offered by the conventional strategic criteria of internal and external fit.

Nevertheless, a battery of tests does not, by itself, identify the roots of sustained superior performance. In this chapter, we review strategic theories about the sources of sustained value creation in light of some of the tests explicit or implicit in earlier chapters of this book. In particular, we focus on three dynamic tests:

- Does the theory offer a coherent account of how added value is built up over time?

- Does it explain how added value can be sustained in the face of imitation threats?

- Does it offer useful insights into how to deal with change, especially fundamental change in the business landscape?

Although we could interpret the last test in terms of substitution threats, in this chapter we prefer to think of change more broadly—as unlocking both opportunities and threats. In landscape imagery, fundamental change can push up new peaks as well as pull down existing ones. The question then becomes: How much help does a strategic theory offer in dealing with such changes, beyond advice to keep climbing the peak that the organization had already begun to scale?

Our three tests are quite general, but we begin by illustrating their usefulness with a specific application: to the ongoing debate about whether tightly coupled activity-systems or valuable resources are the best explanations of sustained success. Our review of this debate suggests a need for more explicitly dynamic thinking. In response to this need, we highlight two ways of thinking about strategic dynamics that we have emphasized separately in the past: making commitments (Ghemawat) and developing capabilities (Pisano). We argue that making commitments and developing capabilities are highly complementary ways of building and sustaining superior performance. An organization's capabilities at any point in time shape the kinds of commitment opportunities it can realistically exploit. At the same time, building capabilities involves a certain degree of irreversibility and thus commitment. To conclude this discussion of strategic dynamics, we briefly summarize what is known about when and how to change strategy.

To fix ideas in what might otherwise become an abstract discussion, we lean heavily on a series of examples of successful companies operating in progressively more turbulent environments: Southwest Airlines, Gillette, and Intel, among others. Although these examples add concreteness to the discussion, they do not cut off all avenues for further debate: That rarely happens in doctrinal matters. As a result, we warn our readers that our attempt to sort through the strategy field in such a short chapter is bound to be somewhat idiosyncratic. Interested readers should therefore refer directly to at least some of the primary sources that we cite, instead of simply relying on our abbreviated rendition of them. And we apologize in advance to readers who may think that their preferred perspectives on strategy are mischaracterized, treated in an offhand way or, worst of all, omitted. Brevity has its risks as well as its rewards.

ACTIVITIES VERSUS RESOURCES

Many researchers in strategic management, when asked to identify the key fault-line in strategy today, might cite the tension between the "activity-system" and "resource-based" views of the firm. As their names indicate, these two theories embody very different opinions about how strategists ought to think about the structures of firms: in terms of the activities that firms perform versus the resources that firms deploy. Although the definitions of these terms tend to be somewhat blurry, "resources" can often be envisioned as stock variables and "activities" as flow variables. It may prove helpful to think of the difference between stocks and flows as being analogous to the difference between companies' balance sheets and their income statements.

Perhaps predictably, the activity-system and resource-based views have fueled a debate about whether activity systems or resources are the *real* roots of sustained superior performance. We refrained from highlighting this divergence in earlier chapters because of our sense that many of the tools and ideas we were developing would be applicable on either side of this divide. It is now time, however, to articulate these two theories of strategy and subject them to our dynamic tests. In addition to sorting through the debate about activities versus resources, the exercise should help illustrate how the value-based logic developed in this book can be used to evaluate the large and growing literature about strategy.

The principal example that we will use to illustrate the differences and similarities between the activity-system view and the resource-based view involves Southwest Airlines. Southwest is the only U.S. airline to have been consistently profitable in the last 25 years, has grown at an annual rate of 20%–30% over the last five years, maintains the youngest fleet and the lowest debt levels among the major carriers, and leads the industry in terms of customer service ratings. This rich example has been studied extensively in the academic literature as well as the business press.[1] It has also been cited as evidence in support of both the activity-system and resource-based views (as well as a host of other theories of value creation based on factors such as vision, insight, and even luck).

The Activity-System View

The systems view of strategy, which focuses on the interdependencies that make up the firm, is one of the staples of the strategy field. Consider, for instance, part of the description of the Business Policy course offered in 1917 at the Harvard Business School:[2]

> An analysis of any business problem shows not only its relation to other problems in the same group, but also the intimate connection of groups. For example, not only is any problem of factory management related to other problems in the factory, and any problem of selling related to other problems in the sales department, but also the groups of problems are interdependent. Few problems in business are purely intra-departmental.

Although the systems view survived World War I (it is evident, for instance, in Kenneth Andrews' pioneering definition of strategy as a pattern in decisions), it has recently been reemphasized in a specific form by Michael Porter's work on activity systems.[3] Porter's argument is three-pronged. First, strategy should be distinguished from "operational effectiveness" (that is, execution), because it involves choosing a fundamentally different set of activities to deliver a unique mix of value rather than performing essentially the same set of activities better than competitors. Second, choices about the activities that are to be performed must fit together to yield a competitive advantage. Third, in Porter's own words, "Strategic fit among many activities is fundamental not only to competitive advantage but also to the sustainability of that advantage."[4]

The first prong of Porter's argument represents an attempt to revive the old distinction between "doing the right things" and "doing things right." We find this attempt to cleanly separate strategy and execution somewhat unconvincing for reasons that will become clearer in the discussion of capability development in the next section of this chapter.[5] We do regard Porter's emphasis on the role of fit in creating competitive advantage as very valuable: It greatly influenced the writing of Chapter 3. Of more interest here, however, is the third prong of Porter's argument: that the inimitability of a successful business model over time is best explained in terms of the cross-sectional linkages among activities. We will explore this prong of the argument, as well as subjecting Porter's theory to the two other dynamic tests cited in the introduction to this chapter: Does the theory offer a coherent account of the process by which added value is built up, and does it offer useful insights into ways of dealing with change, especially fundamental change?

Fortunately for us, Southwest Airlines is one of several examples that Porter uses to illustrate his arguments. Exhibit 5.1 reproduces Porter's map of Southwest's activity system, with the darker circles denoting what he characterizes as "higher-order strategic themes." Porter explains that many of the choices embed-

E X H I B I T   5.1

Southwest Airlines' Activity System (*Source:* Michael E. Porter. "What Is Strategy?" *Harvard Business Review* November–December 1996.)

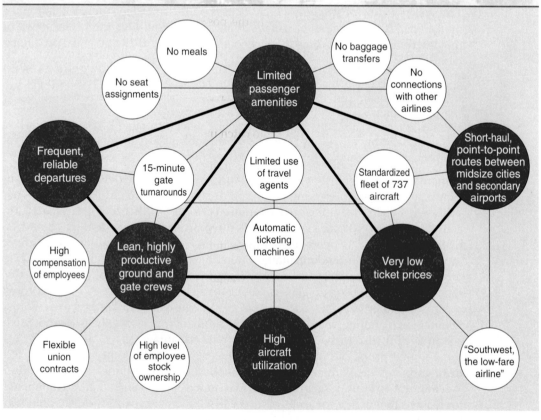

ded in Southwest's activity system are exceptions to, rather than normal practices within, the airline industry. He also describes Continental's unsuccessful attempt to imitate Southwest on a number of point-to-point routes by establishing Continental Lite, a carrier that eliminated first-class service and meals, tried to shorten turnaround times at gates, increased departure frequency, and lowered fares. Continental Lite continued, however, to provide baggage checking, seat assignments, and frequent flyer awards, as well as to use travel agents, because Continental remained a full-service airline on other routes. This hybrid business system quickly proved unviable. Delays due to congestion at hub cities and baggage transfers led to numerous late flights and cancellations. Customers became irked by Continental's decision to reduce the awards on its entire frequent-flier program, as the airline could not offer the same frequent-flier benefits on the much lower Lite fares. Similarly, Continental could not afford to pay standard travel-agent commissions on Lite fares but could not afford to do without travel agents for its full-service business either, so it compromised by cutting commissions across the board. The new operation accumulated hundreds of millions of dollars of losses and eventually had to be grounded.

This example suggests that the interplay of complementarities *and* trade-offs across multiple activities is critical to the possibility of "many best ways to compete," which rests on a rugged landscape marked by multiple peaks.[6] With such multiple peaks, imitation may be limited by potential imitators' decisions to climb different peaks, that is, to compete in different ways. Somewhat surprisingly, however, Porter deemphasizes this solution to the imitation problem. What he emphasizes, instead, is that imitation may be rendered difficult or even impossible when late-movers must match an early-mover along many dimensions, especially if they are interlocked, rather than seeking to catch up along just one or two dimensions.

There *is* some analytical basis to Porter's argument that an activity system that fits together tightly can prove difficult to imitate because of its complexity.[7] In our opinion, however, he overstates his case when he implies that fit among activities is *the* basis for a sustainable competitive advantage. First, the complexity that is supposed to make tightly coupled activity systems hard to imitate focuses attention on just one of the eight barriers to imitation cited in Chapter 4. It is not clear why strategists should narrow their focus in this way if the intent is to think holistically about the problem of imitation.

Second, although imitating many things may indeed take longer, cost more, and afford less certain prospects of success than imitating just one thing, early-mover advantages of some sort are required to explain why—irrespective of the number of activities to be imitated—strategic innovation of complex activity systems might prove to be profitable while strategic imitation is not. The activity-system view offers no help in this regard, because it takes an entirely cross-sectional (that is, atemporal) perspective in dealing with a fundamentally dynamic issue.

Our third dynamic test—Does the theory offer useful insights into how to deal with change?—raises additional questions about the activity-system view that all firms should build tightly coupled activity systems. Tightly coupled activity systems may perhaps prove more agile in responding to relatively small changes but are expected to have a high inertial component when the environment requires many changes.[8] As a result, there has been a recent upsurge of interest in alternatives to tight coupling, such as modular activity systems—that is, systems in which individual activities or clusters of activities (modules) can be changed or replaced without significantly affecting how other activities are carried out or how the system as a whole performs.[9]

Some of the most striking contemporary examples of modularization come, as one might expect, from turbulent environments. For instance, the computer industry has witnessed the technological and organizational decoupling of the design and manufacture of various system components (central processing units, memory, storage systems, peripherals, operating system software, and application software).[10] Likewise, in the pharmaceutical industry, a dramatic increase in the number of technologies used to discover drugs (combinatorial chemistry, genetic engineering, rational drug design, and so on) has led to the decoupling of research and clinical testing, among other activities. While such modularity can lower barriers to imitation and limit fine-tuning across modules, it can also pay for itself by facilitating larger-scale change.

To summarize, the activity-system view seems more useful in thinking about added value or competitive advantage at a point in time than in addressing dynamic issues.

The Resource-Based View

The resource-based view of the firm stresses the importance of looking at firms in terms of the resources that they deploy.[11] This idea is an old one, but was revived in 1984 in an article by Birger Wernerfelt.[12] Wernerfelt, drawing on Andrews, defined resources very broadly, as "anything which could be thought of as a strength or weakness of a given firm."[13] Implicit in this definition was the idea that resources were fixed factors—that is, attributes of the firm that could not be varied in the short run.

Airplanes represent the most obvious fixed factor in the airline business. They also figure prominently in the Southwest example: They help connect most of the dark circles in Exhibit 5.1 and a significant fraction of the light ones. Southwest manages to fly its planes for an average of 11.5 hours per day, compared with 8.6 hours for the industry (even though one might expect lower numbers for Southwest given that its flights tend to be relatively short).[14] Without this resource-utilization advantage, Southwest would need as many as one-third more planes to fly the same number of trips! An emphasis on keeping planes in the air for as much of the day as possible helps explain many of Southwest's policies: avoidance of congested airports, standardization of the fleet around Boeing 737s, no meals or baggage transfers, departures spaced regularly throughout the day, and so on.

A resource-based theorist might regard our ability to explain so many of the elements of Porter's activity map (shown in Exhibit 5.1) in terms of the imperative

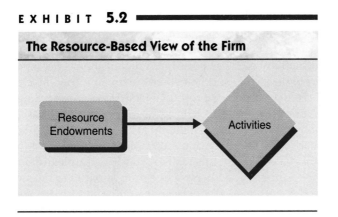

E X H I B I T **5.2**

The Resource-Based View of the Firm

to maximize the utilization of one specific type of resource as evidence that the resource-based view focuses on higher-order strategic choices. To our minds, however, this pattern reflects the complementarity of the resource-based and activity-system views, as depicted in Exhibit 5.2. A firm's resources (stocks) determine the range and the economics of the activities (flows) in which it can engage at any point in time. The product-market implications of those activities, in turn, supply the most obvious basis for evaluating the competitive superiority or inferiority of the firm's resource portfolio.

The importance of activities *and* resources is illustrated, once again, by Southwest's short turnaround times for its airplanes. Some of Southwest's advantage in this regard stems from the fact that it simplifies the activities its personnel perform at the gate by, for instance, eliminating food service and baggage transfer. But Southwest's advantage reflects differences in resource profiles as well. Thus, Southwest employs less information technology but more human resources in the turnaround process than do its rivals.[15] Specifically, Southwest dedicates an operations agent—a "case manager"—to the turnaround of each flight, whereas a competitor such as American Airlines might assign an operations agent to handle 10 to 15 flights at a time. Southwest's pattern of resource deployment reduces turnaround times by facilitating control, coaching and coordination across a range of interdependent activities.

Other resources could also be cited to explain Southwest's success, either individually or through resource interconnectedness. The resource-based view, however, proposes to do more than just shift our attention from a multitude of activities to a multitude of resources. Its logic also steers us toward firm-specific resources as the sources of sustained competitive advantage. Based on this logic, planes themselves are unlikely to serve as the sources of sustained profit differences among airlines because they can be (and often are) bought and sold on reasonably well-functioning markets. Human resources, which were also cited above, are an obvious alternative in the case of Southwest for three reasons: (1) They are firm-specific; (2) labor costs account for a large share of cost added in the airline industry; and (3) labor costs might be expected to loom particularly large for a particularly heavily unionized carrier with low fares and a relatively labor-intensive business model. Despite these constraints, Southwest reports high levels of employee productivity and has been rated one of the best companies to work for in the United States while simultaneously achieving high levels of customer satisfaction and retention. From the resource-based perspective, Southwest might be depicted as blessed in the short run with an endowment of excellent human resources/relationships. The sustainability of added value through such resources rests on a number of the barriers to imitation cited in Chapter 4: learning, contracts/relationships and time lags, as well as strategic complexity.

Applying the resource-based perspective more broadly to the airline industry also reminds us that the firm-specific resources that are key to profitability (or unprofitability) may vary across firms in ways that depend on their strategies or, more specifically, their business models. Consider the six U.S. airlines whose size exceeds that of Southwest. Hubs are the obvious candidate for the status of key resource in their case, because they all emphasize hub-and-spoke rather than point-to-point operation. Although current data on hub profitability remain closely guarded, estimates are available from 1989, before the industry plunged into several years of losses due to a domestic recession. According to one study, the three largest hubs—Chicago, Dallas-Forth Worth, and Atlanta—accounted for nearly 80% of the operating income of the six major airlines in 1989.[16] There are numerous barriers to the imitation of particularly successful hubs including physical uniqueness, long-term contracts for gates and slots, and scale and scope advantages.

The resource-based view has multiple points of contact with our earlier discussion of barriers to imitation, because it recognizes that history matters: That early-mover advantages supply a simple, yet fruitful way of explaining why success may prove sustainable in the face of imitation threats. Another, more technical way of putting this idea is as follows: The resource-based view recognizes intertemporal linkages in a firm's profit function in a way in which the pure activity-system view does not.

Having said that the resource-based view appears to do a good job of explaining how added value can be sustained in the face of imitation threats, we must add two caveats. The pure resource-based view fares less well in terms of our two other dynamic tests: offering a coherent account of how added value is built up, and supplying useful insights into how to deal with change, especially fundamental change.[17] Consider these two problems in turn.

The pure resource-based view discourages detailed consideration of how superior resources might have been built up over time in that it is often too quick to invoke the "intrinsic inimitability" of truly valuable resources. Thus a resource-based theorist might stress the unmanageable social complexity of resources such as "culture" in cases such as Southwest's. Yet surely interesting things can be learned about the deliberate management of human resources, at least in the service sector (which accounts for two-thirds of U.S. GNP), by studying the Southwest example. Specifically, Southwest's policies and practices for managing its human resources include hiring for attitudes rather than skills, emphasizing team-work instead of hierarchy, designing positions—and union contracts—so that employees can perform several jobs if required, offering front-line employees lati-tude to tackle customer needs without recourse to a supervisor, rewarding them for appropriate behavior economically and emotionally (through the sharing of values and information as well as what has been described as a systematic empha-sis on hugging), and even encouraging off-the-job bonding among employees (through joint charitable activities and high rates of intermarriage) to further a sense of "family." [18] These processes are certainly complex, but they have just as certainly been managed.

A second problem with the pure resource-based view derives from its focus on the exploitation of "legacy" resources. Yet the cash-generation potential of the resources that firms have already put into place often accounts for less than one-half or even one-quarter of their market values, especially in the case of industries or firms that are growing rapidly.[19] In the case of Southwest, for example, recent data suggest that the value of resources-in-place is slightly more than one-third of the company's market value.[20] Clearly, the stock market expects Southwest to grow. The most significant strategic issue at Southwest in the late 1990s, however, seems to be that it is running out of room to grow in the "structural hole" in which it started—that is, its traditional shorthaul niche—and has therefore begun to ini-tiate longer-haul operations. Does this strategy make sense, given the changes it may entail to Southwest's traditional business model: the provision of more than peanuts in flight, erosion of the advantage associated with quick turnaround times at the gate, introduction of wide-body planes into a fleet formerly composed only of Boeing 737s, and so on? The resource-based view, with its emphasis on fixed factors, cannot offer much help in handling this question. In other words, the resource-based view is historical but not fully dynamic. Extending it to account for how firms' resource endowments evolve over time is an important task that is taken up in the next section.

DYNAMIC THEORIES

A fully dynamic approach to strategy demands a theory that links not only what the organization did yesterday (that is, in the past) to what it can do well today, but also what it does today to what it can do well tomorrow (that is, in the future). The resource-based view, as noted earlier, focuses on just one of these two links, from the past to the present, and does so in a somewhat restrictive way. In the rest of this chapter, we try to remedy this deficiency by integrating the influence of both present choices and the dead hand of the past on firm performance.

Exhibit 5.3 summarizes our dynamic framework for thinking about strategy in situations in which both management and history matter. This framework attempts to integrate and generalize the activity-system and resource-based views in a way that connects the evolution of firms' resource endowments or opportu-nity sets to the choices, both activity- and resource-related, that they make from

A Dynamic View of the Firm

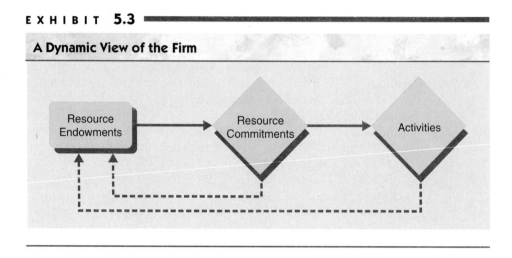

their respective menus of opportunities. The two feedback loops (indicated by the dashed lines in Exhibit 5.3) running from right to left emphasize how the activities that a firm performs and the resource commitments that it makes affect its future resource endowment or opportunity set. The two bold arrows running from left to right suggest two separate points. First, choices about which activities to perform and how to perform them are constrained by resources that can often be varied only in the medium-to-long run. Second, history matters with respect to both long-run resource-related choices and short-run activity-related choices. In other words, the terms on which an organization can make resource commitments and perform activities often depend in important ways on the legacy (that is, the undepreciated residue) of the choices that the organization has made in the past.

Note that the framework depicted in Exhibit 5.3 includes, as special cases, the activity-system view and the resource-based view of the firm. A proponent of activities as the basis of analysis would presumably focus on choices in the last element of Exhibit 5.3; a proponent of resources would concentrate on the first element and how it constrains choices in the last element. Exhibit 5.3 does more than span these two different perspectives, however. It adds value by identifying two ways of building sustainable advantages: by making lumpy resource *commitments* and by purposefully orchestrating the activities that the firm performs, a more incremental process that is often referred to in terms of developing *capabilities*. Investments in both commitments and capabilities can, because of their irreversible nature, lead to the emergence and persistence of firm-specific advantages (or disadvantages). But given the different structures of choices about them— lumpy versus spread out—we will discuss them separately.[21]

Instead of speculating about Southwest Airlines' fate as it tries to expand out of its niche (relatively short flights), we will use the history of Gillette, a company that *has* significantly altered its resource endowments over time, to illustrate our discussion of the importance of making commitments and developing capabilities. The use of a single example is meant to suggest that commitments and capabilities are often intertwined: Firms with above-average capabilities are likely to be able to make commitments with higher expected returns and lower risk than their rivals, and commitments can jump-start the more incremental development of capabilities.

Making Commitments

By commitments, we mean to refer to a few lumpy decisions involving large changes in resource endowments—such as acquiring another company, developing and launching a "breakthrough" product, engaging in a major capacity expansion, and so on—that have significant, lasting effects on firms' future menus of opportunities or choices.[22] The irreversibility of such major decisions or, equivalently, the costs of changing one's mind about them mandates a deep look into the future for reasons that have been articulated particularly well by Robert Townsend, the former CEO of Avis:

> A decision to build the Edsel or Mustang (or locate your new factory in Orlando or Yakima) shouldn't be made hastily; nor without plenty of inputs . . . [But there is] no point in taking three weeks to make a decision that can be made in three seconds—and corrected inexpensively later if wrong. The whole organization may be out of business while you oscillate between baby-blue or buffalo-brown coffee cups.[23]

A somewhat more recent illustration of a major commitment is supplied by Gillette's launch of its Sensor shaving system in January 1990.[24] The launch of Sensor was the linchpin in a strategy to revitalize a company that had been the target of numerous hostile takeover attempts in the second half of the 1980s and that had ended up with negative book equity as a result of defending itself. The launch cost Gillette more than $75 million in R&D (starting in the 1970s), $100 million in manufacturing investments, and $100 million in advertising. As the company sank more money into the project, it accumulated resources whose value was specialized to support the launch. These resources created a presumption in favor of proceeding with the launch, because they had few other obvious uses or users. More generally, lock-in, in the form of sunk costs, is the first source of irreversibility that underlies our concept of commitment.

A second source of irreversibility, lock-out, is the mirror image of lock-in: It results from opportunity costs rather than sunk costs. It can be illustrated with an earlier product launch that Gillette delayed, to its detriment. At the beginning of the 1960s, Gillette trailed Wilkinson, Schick, and American Safety Razor in introducing stainless steel blades, for a number of reasons: Its carbon steel Super Blue blade (introduced in 1960) was doing well; stainless steel blades threatened to reduce the price-per-shave since they lasted three or more times as long as carbon steel blades; and Gillette continued to search for additional technological improvements. But as demand for stainless steel blades soared because of the closer shaves that they provided, Gillette had to scramble to enter that product category. Aided by competitors' production problems, it quickly managed to achieve category leadership. Nevertheless, its worldwide market share in double-edged blades was estimated to have dropped from 90% to 70% as a result of the delay.[25]

This example illustrates that commitment isn't just another synonym for investment: Opportunity costs can lead to just as much irreversibility as sunk costs. More generally, lock-out effects can persist because of the difficulties of reactivating dormant resources, reacquiring discarded resources, or recreating lapsed opportunities to deploy particular resources in particular ways. Both lock-in and lock-out possibilities must be examined to determine whether a particular decision represents a major commitment.

How should we evaluate commitments? The tests of value developed in the last two chapters help us achieve greater rigor than simple injunctions to "think big." Reconsider the example of Gillette's Sensor razor. Because of the fixed costs associated with launching the new shaving system and the higher variable costs of producing Sensor cartridges, the launch decision essentially hinged on whether enough customers would be willing to pay 6 cents for a shave with a Sensor, compared with approximately 5 cents for Gillette's Atra shaving system and 3.5 cents or less for disposable blades. Assuming that customers would be willing to pay more for a smoother shave, imitation did not pose much of a threat. Although antitrust concerns led Gillette to make its 22 patents on Sensor available to competitors, competitors did not even attempt to imitate this product, presumably because of their inferior process-development capabilities (as described later in this chapter). Substitution threats actually favored the launch. Gillette's cartridge business in the United States, in particular, had been losing two to three percentage points of market share each year to lower-margin disposables. The prospect of halting this trend constituted one of the major attractions in launching Sensor as aggressively as Gillette did. Of course, the new product proved unexpectedly profitable because it actually reversed the trend toward disposables instead of simply curtailing it.

It is also worth emphasizing that the value-based tests developed in the previous two chapters have some teeth: They don't automatically rubberstamp all commitments that are actually undertaken. Consider Gillette's launch of its Mach 3 generation of shaving systems in 1998—its first quantum commitment to the shaving business since the introduction of Sensor. Gillette spent more than three times as much—approximately $1 billion—launching a new, triple-blade technology with Mach 3 as it did in moving from conventional twin blades (Atra) to spring-mounted twin blades (Sensor). Gillette's stock market value, however, declined by more than $2 billion on the day that Mach 3 was announced. Value-based tests help explain concerns about this launch. First, at Gillette's recommended number of shaves per cartridge, the retail price has increased to 10-plus cents per shave. Are consumers willing to pay this amount? Second, Gillette's recommended number of shaves may well be exceeded because of Mach 3's new "diamond-like coating." Although such increases in product durability improve affordability, they also shrink the number of units sold. Third, from a dynamic standpoint, the picture is more mixed than in the case of Sensor: Although Mach 3 will probably prove even more difficult to imitate, it doesn't help combat a serious substitution threat. Instead, it will mostly cannibalize sales of Sensor Excel (the upgraded version of Sensor), which were already highly profitable.

The prospect that Mach 3 might destroy rather than create value for Gillette reminds us that lumpy strategic commitments are too important to be subordinated to the existing strategy: They must be analyzed in depth because they represent important checkpoints at which an organization must be prepared to reevaluate its entire strategy. Based on its launch patterns since the 1960s, Gillette appears to have adopted the principle of pacing its product innovation efforts so as to introduce a major new shaving system at least once every 10 years.[26] Thus, some observers expect the next new shaving system to be introduced in 2006, eight years after the launch of Mach 3, which came eight years after Sensor.[27] While it may indeed be desirable to impose a certain rhythm on product development schedules, this rhythm cannot be decided upon in a vacuum. Instead, it must be synchronized with opportunities and threats in the business landscape—and adjusted to changes in those conditions—if it is to maximize value.

Commitment theory certainly offers a coherent account of how added value is built up over time (although capability development often plays a complementary role, as discussed in the next section). Commitments also play a key role in creating the barriers to imitation that were discussed in Chapter 4 since most of these barriers rest on some underlying source of irreversibility. The most challenging question that can be raised about the theory of commitment concerns our third dynamic test: Does it offer helpful insights into how to deal with change, particularly fundamental change? At one level, the answer is clearly "yes": Shaping and even adapting to fundamental change usually require major commitments. At another level, however, things are less clear: Change is usually accompanied by uncertainty, which emerges as a particularly important issue in the context of commitments, given their extreme irreversibility.

The difficulty of predicting with perfect certainty whether commitments (such as the launch of the Mach 3 shaving system) will turn out to be good or bad has given rise to a large body of literature on how to incorporate uncertainty into their analysis that yields some very useful lessons.

First, commitments can lead to persistently inferior performance (if they fail) as well as sustained superior performance.

Second, we must recognize the multiplicity of possible outcomes if we are to address uncertainty effectively. This need usually requires the construction of multiple scenarios rather than the shoehorning of all risk into a discount or hurdle rate.

Third, although uncertainty can sometimes increase the attractiveness of alternatives to making commitments, such as investing in less specialized resources, hedging one's bets, or delaying action, it rarely pays to try to stay *totally* flexible: That choice would increase lock-out risks, reduce a company's ability to influence the resolution of uncertainty, and result in mediocre performance at best.

Fourth, the problem of commitment under conditions of uncertainty is lessened by the fact that many commitment-intensive choices afford high "learn-to-burn ratios." Such a ratio is defined as the rate at which information is received about whether a commitment is turning out to be a plum or a lemon divided by the rate at which sunk or opportunity costs are incurred in pursuing it. High learn-to-burn ratios provide timely feedback in a way that permits revisions of commitments in response to bad news—an important source of option value in an uncertain world.

Fifth, realization of the potential for high learn-to-burn ratios requires careful management and can be enhanced in a variety of ways—by experimenting, engaging in pilot programs, appropriately staging or sequencing commitments, setting milestones and triggers for terminating commitment to a losing course of action, ensuring that appropriate incentives are in place, and so on.

Finally, one of the most powerful approaches for dealing with the uncertainty is to develop superior capabilities that increase the odds of success and let the firm "fall forward" rather than backward in response to the unanticipated challenges that inevitably arise in the course of making major commitments. Capability development is discussed next.

Developing Capabilities

The development of capabilities involves choices that are individually small and frequent rather than individually important and infrequent. In terms of Exhibit 5.3, capabilities can be associated with the feedback loop that runs from activities to resource endowments. The idea is that firm-specific capabilities to perform activities better than competitors can be built gradually and reinforced over long periods of time. Note that the dynamic capabilities view of the firm differs from the resource-based view in that capabilities must be developed rather than being taken as given, as described more fully in an article by David Teece, Gary Pisano, and Amy Shuen:

> If control over scarce resources is the source of economic profits, then it follows that issues such as skill acquisition and learning become fundamental strategic issues. It is this second dimension, encompassing skill acquisition, learning, and capability accumulation that . . . [we] refer to as "the dynamic capabilities approach" . . . Rents are viewed as not only resulting from uncertainty . . . but also from directed activities by firms which create differentiated capabilities, and from managerial efforts to strategically deploy these assets in coordinated ways.[28]

Taking dynamic capabilities seriously also implies that one of the firm's most strategic aspects is "the way things are done in the firm, or what might be referred to as its 'routines,' or patterns of current practice and learning."[29] As a result, "research in such areas as management of R&D, product and process development, manufacturing, and human resources tend to be quite relevant [to strategy]."[30] Such research supplies some specific content to the idea that strategy execution is important.

Gillette provides a good example of a company that has built up superior manufacturing capabilities over time. It managed to come from behind in coated stainless steel blades because it was able to ramp up production much more quickly than its rivals. The most formidable barrier to the imitation of Sensor appears to have been the process expertise required to develop laser-welding technology (which was previously used only for low-volume applications such as heart pacemakers) for a very-high-volume application—reaching almost 100 welds per second with a production reject rate of only 10 blades per million. With Mach 3, Gillette has raised the bar even higher; based on its investment of $750 million in continuous-motion production lines and advanced robotics, it hopes to triple its production rates—despite the Mach 3's more complex design.

Major commitments to process development and new machinery are partly responsible for the advances that Gillette has recorded over time, but it is also easy to imagine other companies spending as much as Gillette did without achieving comparable breakthroughs. Systematic research across a range of other settings documents large differences in organizational capabilities that cannot be explained by differences in spending. Such capabilities encompass not only product and process development, but also marketing skills, the capacity to learn and adapt, the ability to integrate across functions, and a host of other dimensions.[31]

On the basis of this research, it appears that superior capabilities can indeed lead to superior performance, by improving the terms on which activities can be performed or resource commitments made. To achieve this goal, a firm's capability along a particular dimension must truly be competitively superior. This seems relatively obvious in the case of Gillette's manufacturing capabilities. In most cases, however, competitive superiority in terms of differences in cost, willingness to pay, adaptability, and other areas must be tested objectively. In the absence of an objective test, hubris and politics are likely to lead to excessively high self-ratings and a tendency to designate anything that one cares about as a key organizational capability. (An analogous problem arises in the identification of key resources or core competences.) As a result, capabilities must usually be benchmarked competitively, even if the process yields incomplete results.

If a firm is to sustain superior performance, its capabilities must be difficult to imitate as well as competitively superior. In other words, they must satisfy our second dynamic test as well as our first one. The barriers to imitation that capability theorists most often invoke involve learning, time lags, complexity, and upgrading. In particular, they often characterize learning as being rooted in detailed and complex organizational processes that span many individuals, may link multiple firms, and are often difficult for competitors to observe. Such learning cumulates in a pool of knowledge that tends to be the most firm-specific and inimitable when it is tacit rather than specifiable (that is, can't be blueprinted) and when it is collectively held by members of the organization rather than being available to any one or two employees to walk away with. Note that knowledge *can* be managed in ways that make it less likely to spill over to competitors. Thus, in preparing to launch Mach 3, Gillette parceled out work in building components of the production lines among several dozen machine shops, erected high plywood walls inside its factory to conceal the production lines, restricted access to this area to employees with special electronic badges, constantly reminded workers of the need for secrecy (banning discussions of the new product, even with employees' spouses), and brought in the Federal Bureau of Investigation to help plug leaks.[32]

Capabilities that can sustain superior performance typically remain somewhat specific to particular uses as well as firms. Compare, in this respect, the capabilities that supported Gillette's launch of Sensor with the ones that were supposed to underpin Gannett's decision, in 1981, to launch another widely available consumer product, the *USA Today* newspaper.[33] Ten years later, the new national newspaper had accumulated losses of $800 million, not accounting for the time-value of money, and was still operating in the red. Although many reasons underlie *USA Today*'s financial failure, some of them seem related to the fact that the capabilities and resources that were supposed to make it attractive for Gannett to launch a national newspaper were fairly generic: They included a reputation for being one of the five best-managed companies in the United States, editorial expertise (albeit only with local newspapers), and cash. Compared with the deep technological, manufacturing, marketing, and distribution capabilities that Gillette had built up by the time of Sensor's launch, Gannett's capabilities appear about as shallow as they were broad.

Having made the point that no all-purpose capabilities exist, we should recognize that capabilities do differ in terms of their usage-specificity in interesting ways. In an uncertain, changing world—the challenge highlighted by our third dynamic test—it may be worth paying some attention to breadth as well as depth; that is, it may prove fruitful to place some emphasis on "mobility" or usage-flexibility instead of simply deepening usage-specific capabilities and thereby increasing rigidity.[34] Microsoft, for instance, has been able to transform itself into a major player in Internet browsers and applications and networking software in response to the substitution threat posed by the emergence of the Internet to desktop computing. This move reflects not only Microsoft's strong-arm tactics, but also its "basic," somewhat mobile capabilities to engineer and manage the development of massively complex software systems.

Mobility appears to be enhanced by the breadth of a company's knowledge base. It has been argued, for example, that Canon's successful transition across several discontinuities in photolithography equipment (used in semiconductor production) was rooted in emphasis on "architectural knowledge," or broad knowledge about component technologies *and* their interactions.[35] A study of 440 of the most technologically active companies in the world goes so far as to conclude that

> Management in large firms needs to sustain a broader (*if less deep*) set of technological competencies in order to coordinate *continuous improvement and innovation* in the corporate production system and supply chain.[36]

Although clear limits exist to constrain the scope of a firm's technological capabilities (including the danger of ending up "subscale" in each technology), a certain amount of breadth can sometimes prove helpful.

Having noted this theoretical trade-off between deeper capabilities and broader mobility, we must add that many organizations could potentially improve on both fronts, if only the processes used to manage them—in terms of resource allocation mechanisms, organizational structure, patterns of hiring, compensation and promotion, and so on—were more appropriate. To take just one example, Christensen has used evidence from the disk drive industry to argue that, when an organization's resource allocation processes are too tightly tied to its *existing* base of customers and their needs, it is likely to miss opportunities to develop technologies that initially only meet the requirements of a different customer base.[37] By implication, management can help improve the trade-off between breadth and depth that an organization actually faces.

To wrap up this discussion, we should issue a warning about the apparently incremental nature of most attempts at capability (or mobility) development. Firms that seek to develop superior capabilities as the basis of sustainable competitive advantages must prevent the overall coherence of their capability development efforts from being nibbled away, choice by choice, by drop-in-the-bucket biases and the like. As a result, the choice of which capabilities to develop, and how to develop them, becomes a somewhat lumpy choice—like the major commitments discussed earlier. The similarity makes sense when one notes that a capability development thrust has the same lock-in and lock-out effects associated with conventionally lumpy commitment decisions.

THE CHALLENGE OF CHANGE

The challenge of change may already have crystallized in some readers' minds as the latent theme of this chapter, given that we have used it (in the form of our third dynamic test) to gain some perspective on activities, resources, commitments, and capabilities. In regard to the activity-system view, the challenge of fundamental change forced us to note the arguments for modular rather than tightly coupled activity systems. The pure resource-based view had little to say about fundamental change, beyond the insight that as the environment changes, an organization may—in some instances—want to develop its new strategy around the resources in its endowment that are the most difficult to alter. The two dynamic extensions of the resource-based view, making commitments and developing capabilities, helped us address changes in resources over time, but had to be qualified with discussions of a range of flexibility/mobility enhancers.

These qualifications were essential because we usually think of building and sustaining superior performance as climbing to the top of (or part way up) a particular peak on the business landscape. With changing business landscapes, however, knowing when to change the peak you are climbing may be as important as climbing toward a particular peak. In this section, we attempt to synthesize this point of view, instead of dealing with it in piecemeal fashion (as we did in the last two sections).

We begin by distinguishing between two extreme types of business landscapes, and the types of strategies that can make sense within them. At one extreme, we might imagine a stable landscape in which the future is relatively certain. We would expect successful organizations to exhibit strategic continuity within such landscapes—that is, to focus on climbing a particular peak but to search continuously for improvements within that fixed set of initial conditions. Ghemawat and Ricart i Costa have referred to this organizational mindset as the search for static efficiency.[38] At the other extreme, we can imagine a landscape that is so turbulent as to verge on the chaotic, in which the future is truly ambiguous. There, we might expect organizations to continuously entertain changes in their strategies—that is, to focus on continuously reconsidering initial conditions, or which peak to climb. Ghemawat and Ricart i Costa have called this organizational mindset the search for dynamic efficiency.

This distinction gains its usefulness from the fact that some tension appears to arise between organizational arrangements that promote static efficiency (or local learning) and those that promote dynamic efficiency. Exhibit 5.4 illustrates this tension: it tries to distinguish between organizational archetypes on the basis of whether they involve "current efficiency and regularity" (static efficiency) or "innovation and flexibility" (dynamic efficiency).[39] To the extent that it is hard to mix and match across the two columns in Exhibit 5.4—for example, because different types of employees are required—that tension is likely to lead to "tipping" toward extremes. Organizations may therefore face pressure to choose between two very different archetypes.

Extreme choices are most satisfactory in the two extreme types of business landscapes mentioned above. They are less satisfactory when we must deal with intermediate cases, in which the business landscape is neither continuously stable nor chaotic. Such landscapes appear to account for the majority of all cases. Intermediate levels of change and uncertainty seem responsible, for instance, for the fact that strategies, instead of exhibiting continuity or continuous change, generally follow a pattern known as punctuated equilibria; in this pattern, strategic continuity is the norm, but is punctuated by brief periods of radical change (see Exhibit 5.5).[40] Punctuated equilibria arise from both internal factors (patterns of organizational growth and evolution that require discontinuous change) and external factors (particularly technological cycles, in which "dematuring" technological shocks are followed by technological maturation—a shift from product to process innovation and a general decrease in the rate of innovation—until the next shock comes along).

Successful navigation of such cycles requires mastery of both evolutionary and revolutionary change. This steering process is inherently challenging because of the tensions between the two strategies outlined in Exhibit 5.4. Yet many leading-edge organizations regard this challenge as critical to their ability to sustain success. Tushman and O'Reilly have elaborated on the challenge of combining static and dynamic conceptions of efficiency:

> The real test of leadership, then, is to be able to compete successfully by both increasing the alignment or fit among strategy, structure, culture, and processes, while simultaneously preparing for the inevitable revolutions required by discontinuous environmental change. This requires organizational and management skills to compete in a mature market (where cost, efficiency, and incremental innovation are key) *and* to develop new products and services (where radical innovation, speed, and flexibility are critical).[41]

EXHIBIT 5.4

Aligning Elements of Strategy (*Source:* Excerpted from Heskett, op. cit.)

	Summary of Strategy Developed for Current Efficiency and Regularity	Summary of Strategy Developed for Innovation and Flexibility
Resources		
Human	Emphasis on qualities of compliance and commitment	Emphasis on qualities of originality and commitment
Financial	Growth financed largely from ongoing business	Significant development investment requiring financial capacity
Technological	Emphasis on incremental product and process improvements	Emphasis on the development of entirely new products and basic new technologies
Organization		
Structure	Centralized/functional orientation Clear vertical chain of authority for decisions/communication Sales and/or operations as the dominant functions	Decentralized/product orientation Network of influence and communication Utilize projects and task forces Marketing and/or R&D as the dominant functions
Controls	Tight, detailed plans and budgets Reviews at short intervals	Loose planning around objectives (management by objectives)
Standards	Specific individual or group targets Compete with internal comparisons "Stretch" goals defined in terms of sales or production levels	General targets Compete with external comparisons "Stretch" goals defined in terms of project delivery dates
Rewards	Tie rewards to individual or group performance Promote for making plans	Tie rewards to total business performance Promote for innovative results Reward risk-takers with "soft landing" for failure
Policies/processes	Top-down decision-making process Establish clear career tracks	Bottom-up and top-down decision-making processes Use a clear "maze"
Working environment	Pride in Marine-like precision Emphasis on making your numbers in terms of costs, delivery, and quality Regular working hours and dress	Pride in being first with bright ideas Emphasis on creative teamwork Working hours and dress to meet individual preferences

Tushman and O'Reilly also think that they have found organizations that have institutionalized ways of surmounting the twin challenges of evolutionary and revolutionary change. They cite three exemplars in this regard—Hewlett-Packard, Johnson & Johnson, and Asea Brown Boveri (ABB)—as sharing certain common characteristics:[42]

- Massive decentralization of decision making, but with consistency attained through individualized accountability, information sharing, and strong financial

EXHIBIT **5.5**

Patterns of Strategic Change

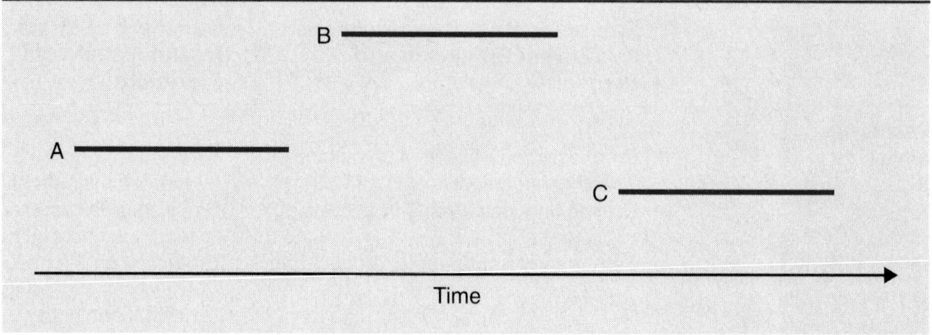

Time

---

control. But why doesn't this result in fragmentation and a loss of synergy? The answer is found in the use of social control.

- Reliance on strong social controls . . . [that] are simultaneously tight and loose. They are tight in that the corporate culture in each is broadly shared and emphasizes norms critical for innovation such as openness, autonomy, initiative, and risk taking. The culture is loose in that the manner in which these common values are expressed varies according to the type of innovation [or change] required.

- Ambidextrous managers managing units that pursue widely different strategies and that have varied structures and cultures . . . The corporate vision provides the compass by which senior managers can make decisions about which of the many alternative businesses and technologies to invest in, but the market is the ultimate arbiter of winners and losers.

Whether most organizations or managers can aspire to become ambidextrous in the sense of simultaneously managing evolutionary and revolutionary change remains an open issue. Andy Grove, the chairman of Intel, provides an interesting and richly textured view from the trenches that is more sequential than simultaneous. He assumes that in well-functioning organizations, most managers do the right things most of the time and zeroes in on the times when the usual practice of management is likely to work least well, which he calls strategic inflection points:

> A strategic inflection point is a time in the life of a business when its fundamentals are about to change. That change can mean an opportunity to rise to new heights. But it may just as likely signal the beginning of the end.[43]

Examples of strategic inflection points for his own company that are cited by Grove include the Japanese DRAM producers' invasion of Intel's memory business in the mid-1980s, the floating-point problem that surfaced with Intel's Pentium processor in late 1994, and, more recently, the emergence of the Internet and the sub-$1,000 personal computer.

Grove also stresses the barriers to recognizing and reacting to strategic inflection points in time and the tools needed to enhance a firm's likelihood of achieving that goal. His list of barriers includes generally low signal-to-noise ratios, a natural human impulse to deny change (especially when change is painful), disincentives (determined at the top) to adapt to or take advantage of fundamental change, dithering/deadlocks, and a leadership that may itself risk becoming obsolete because of the changes (in skill sets and mindsets) that are required. His list of performance enhancers includes bringing together people with "knowledge power" and those with "organizational power," vigorous and frank debate without any fallout from advancing contrarian opinions, careful observation of changes in the behavior of other key players, and the use of improved analytical frameworks (for example, the value net rather than the "five forces" framework in the case of Intel). Finally, Grove argues that once an organization does conclude that it has reached a strategic inflection point, its leader needs to figure out what the organization will and will not do (what many call "vision," although Grove rejects the term as being too lofty), and then lead it through the "valley of death" to climb the new peak thereby implied.

We think that Grove's point is an appropriately clear and crisp depiction of managerial action with which to end this chapter. Much of managerial action—not just strategy—involves trying to climb particular peaks by linking activities, developing capabilities, and making commitments. Most long-lived organizations must, however, periodically reconsider the peaks that they are climbing. As a result, managers need to know when to hold on to their strategy and when to let go. Making that decision is, in a sense, the meta-strategic challenge.

SUMMARY

This chapter reviewed strategic theories about the sources of sustained value creation in light of the tests developed in earlier chapters of this book. It concluded that the activity-system and the resource-based views of the firm are complementary, but need to be extended dynamically to account for the ways in which managers can shape the evolution of their firms' resource endowments over time. Making commitments and developing capabilities offer ways to satisfy that need for dynamization.

This chapter also emphasized, however, that making commitments or developing capabilities is no more of a strategic panacea than building tightly coupled activity systems or concentrating on key resources. The reason is related to the ongoing tension between the irreversibility of firms' choices and changes in the landscapes on which they operate. As a result, choices concerning activities, resources, commitments, and capabilities must be examined in depth, with an eye toward the tests of economic value developed in this book.

Finally and most deeply, the discussion in this chapter should have illustrated ways of evaluating the large and growing literature about strategy. Ideas about strategy continue to appear (and disappear) at rapid, probably increasing rates. The value-based logic developed in this book supplies a basis for distinguishing between new ideas that are likely to be valuable and those that are not. We think that to be the most valuable contribution that a book such as this one can make.

GLOSSARY

activity-system view	lock-in
capabilities	lock-out
change	mobility
commitments	modular activity systems
complementarities	option value
dynamic efficiency	punctuated equilibria
firm-specific resources	resource-based view
fixed factors	routines
irreversibility	static efficiency
learn-to-burn ratios	strategic inflection points
legacy resources	trade-offs

NOTES

1. See, for example, James L. Heskett, W. Earl Sasser, Jr., and Leonard A. Schlesinger, *The Service Profit Chain: How Leading Companies Link Profit and Growth to Loyalty, Satisfaction and Value* (New York: Free Press, 1997), and Jody H. Gittell, "Coordinating Service Across Functional Boundaries: The Departure Process at Southwest Airlines," Harvard Business School Working Paper No. 98-050. Other sources will be cited as appropriate.

2. Harvard University. *Official Register, Graduate School of Business Administration* (March 1917), pp. 42–43. We are indebted to Jan Rivkin for this citation.

3. See Kenneth R. Andrews, *The Concept of Corporate Strategy* (Homewood, IL: Richard D. Irwin, 1971) and Michael E. Porter, "What Is Strategy?," *Harvard Business Review* November–December 1996: 61–78. For impressive recent research contributions to the systems view, consult Jan W. Rivkin, "Consequences of Fit," unpublished Ph.D. dissertation, Harvard University, 1997, and Nicolaj

Siggelkow, "Benefits of Focus, Evolution of Fit, and Agency Issues in the Mutual Fund Industry," unpublished Ph.D. dissertation, Harvard University, 1998.

4. Porter, *op. cit.*, p. 73.

5. Amar Bhide has also pointed out the following logical argument: it is hard to imagine how a firm can execute efficiently—that is, perform similar activities better than its rivals—without performing them in at least slightly different ways.

6. With complementarities alone, the business landscape would be single-peaked—that is, only one best way to compete would exist. This is the situation studied by Paul Milgrom and John Roberts, "The Economics of Modern Manufacturing: Technology, Strategy, and Organization," *American Economic Review,* Vol. 80, 1990: pp. 511–528.

7. See, in particular, the essays in Jan W. Rivkin, *op. cit.*

8. Nicolaj Siggelkow, *op. cit.*, pp. 52–53.

9. See Ron Sanchez, "Strategic Flexibility in Product Competition," *Strategic Management Journal,* Vol.

16, 1995, pp. 135–159. Note that other authors refer to the same broad set of ideas in terms of "chunking" or "patching."

10. Carliss Y. Baldwin and Kim B. Clark, *Design Rules* (Boston: Harvard Business School Press, forthcoming).

11. For an early review of this literature that is still valuable, see Kathleen R. Conner. "A Historical Comparison of Resource-Based Theory and Five Schools of Thought within Industrial Organization Economics: Do We Have a New Theory of the Firm?" *Journal of Management* 1991, 1:121–154.

12. See Edith T. Penrose, *The Theory of the Growth of the Firm* (Oxford: Basil Blackwell, 1959), and Birger Wernerfelt, "A Resource-Based View of the Firm," *Strategic Management Journal* 1984; 5:171–180.

13. Wernerfelt, *op. cit.,* p. 172.

14. See Kevin Freiberg and Jackie Freiberg, *Nuts!: Southwest Airlines' Crazy Recipe for Business and Personal Success* (Austin: Bard Press, 1996), p. 51.

15. Jody H. Gittell, "Coordinating Service Across Functional Boundaries: The Departure Process at Southwest Airlines," Harvard Business School Working Paper No. 98-050.

16. The study was conducted by a major strategy consulting firm that would prefer to remain anonymous.

17. By the "pure" resource-based view, we intend to refer to work that stresses the fixity of key firm-specific resources. Jay B. Barney's "Firm Resources and Sustained Competitive Advantage," *Journal of Management* (March 1991), pp. 99–120, is an example. Resource-based writings that recognize the importance of upgrading key resources come much closer in spirit to the more dynamic perspective that we advocate in the next section. See, for instance, David J. Collis and Cynthia A. Montgomery, "Competing on Resources: Strategy in the 1990s," *Harvard Business Review* (July-August 1995), pp. 118–128.

18. These policies are all reviewed by James L. Heskett, W. Earl Sasser, Jr., and Leonard A. Schlesinger in *The Service Profit Chain* (New York: Free Press, 1997). Like many other writers focused purely on execution, however, Heskett *et al.* do not connect to or even recognize the theory of barriers to imitation.

19. W. Carl Kester. "Today's Options for Tomorrow's Growth." *Harvard Business Review* March–April 1984:153–160.

20. This calculation uses the same methodology as Kester, *op. cit.,* and a 15% discount rate.

21. Our emphasis of this distinction distinguishes our attempt to dynamize the resource-based view from other efforts to do so, such as the theory of core competences.

22. For a book-length discussion of how to make commitments that expands on many of the ideas mentioned in this section, see Pankaj Ghemawat, *Commitment* (New York: Free Press, 1991). For an article-length summary, see "Commitment: An Interview with Pankaj Ghemawat," *McKinsey Quarterly,* 1992, No. 3, pp. 121–137.

23. Robert Townsend. *Up the Organization* (New York: Knopf, 1970), p. 49.

24. The Gillette example is largely based on Benjamin Esty and Pankaj Ghemawat. "Gillette's Launch of Sensor." ICCH No. 9-792-028. Other sources are cited as appropriate.

25. Gordon McKibben. *Cutting Edge* (Boston: Harvard Business School Press, 1998), p. 58.

26. The major exception occurred during the decade of the 1980s, when the most significant introduction was the upgrade, in 1985, of the Atra razor (originally launched in 1977).

27. William Symonds. "Gillette's Edge." *Business Week* January 19, 1998:70.

28. David J. Teece, Gary Pisano, and Amy Shuen. "Dynamic Capabilities and Strategic Management." Mimeograph, June 1992, pp. 12–13.

29. David Teece and Gary Pisano. "The Dynamic Capabilities of Firms: An Introduction." *Industrial and Corporate Change* 1994; 3:540–541. The idea of "routines" as a unit of analysis was pioneered by Richard R. Nelson and Sidney G. Winter. *An Evolutionary Theory of Economic Change* (Cambridge, MA: Harvard University Press, 1982).

30. David J. Teece, Gary Pisano, and Amy Shuen. "Dynamic Capabilities and Strategic Management." Mimeograph, June 1992, p. 2.

31. Various studies have documented significant differences in productivity across firms in the same industry. To focus just on manufacturing and technology, there have been significant strands of work on (1) manufacturing productivity [for example, Robert H. Hayes and Kim B. Clark. "Exploring the Sources of Productivity Differences at the Factory Level." In: Kim B. Clark, Robert H. Hayes, and Christopher Lorenz, eds. *The Uneasy Alliance: Managing the Productivity-Technology Dilemma* (Boston, MA: Harvard Business School Press, 1985); and James Womack, Daniel Jones, and D. Roos. *The Machine That Changed the World* (New York: Macmillan, 1990)]; (2) product quality [(David A. Garvin. *Managing Quality* (New York: Free Press, 1988)]; (3) manufacturing flexibility (David M.

Upton. "Flexibility as Process Mobility: The Management of Plant Capabilities for Quick Response Manufacturing." *Journal of Operations Management* 1995:205–224); (4) R&D productivity (Rebecca M. Henderson and Ian Cockburn. "Scale, Scope, and Spillovers: The Determinants of Research Productivity in Drug Discovery." *RAND Journal of Economics* Spring 1996; 27:32–60); and (5) product and process development speed and efficiency [Kim B. Clark and Takahiro Fujimoto. *Product Development Performance: Strategy, Organization, and Management in the World Auto Industry* (Boston, MA: Harvard Business School Press, 1991); Gary Pisano. *The Development Factory* (Harvard Business School Press, 1996); and Marco Iansiti. *Technology Integration* (Harvard Business School Press, 1997)].

32. Mark Maremont. "A Cut Above?" *Wall Street Journal* April 14, 1998.

33. Most of the information on *USA Today* is based on Scott Garell and Pankaj Ghemawat, "USA Today Decision (A)," ICCH No. 792-030, and the follow-up (B) case, ICCH No. 792-031.

34. Dorothy Leonard-Barton, in "Core Capabilities and Core Rigidities: A Paradox in Managing New Product Development," *Strategic Management Journal*, Vol. 13, 1992, pp. 111–125, has emphasized that with usage-specificity, core capabilities can become core rigidities. David M. Upton, in "Flexibility as Process Mobility: The Management of Plant Capabilities for Quick Response Manufacturing," *Journal of Operations Management*, 1995, pp. 205–224, discusses the concept of "mobility" in the context of operations, where it refers to the speed with which an operation can shift production from one type of product or service to another. Pankaj Ghemawat and Patricio del Sol, in "Commitment versus Flexibility?," *California Management Review*, Vol. 40 (Summer 1998), pp. 26–42, discuss similar issues in a strategic context and point that out firm-specific resources need not be usage-specific.

35. Rebecca Henderson, "Successful Japanese Giants: Investment in Architectural Knowledge as a Strategic Choice," unpublished working paper, Massachusetts Institute of Technology (May 1992).

36. Ove Granstrand, Pari Patel, and Keith Pavitt, "Multi-Technology Corporations: Why They Have 'Distributed' rather than 'Distinctive Core' Competences," California Management Review, Vol. 39 (Summer 1997), pp. 8–25.

37. See Clayton M. Christensen, *The Innovator's Dilemma* (Boston: Harvard Business School Press, 1997) as well as the discussion of substitution threats in chapter 4.

38. See Pankaj Ghemawat and Joan Ricart i Costa, "The Organizational Tension between Static and Dynamic Efficiency," *Strategic Management Journal*, Vol. 14, 1993, pp. 59–73, for formalization and analysis of the concepts of static and dynamic efficiency.

39. James L. Heskett, "Establishing Strategic Direction: Aligning Elements of Strategy," ICCH No. 9-388-033. While several rows of Heskett's original table have been omitted, it has not otherwise been modified.

40. For evidence of such patterns of change in strategies, see Danny Miller and Peter Friesen, *Organizations: A Quantum View* (Englewood Cliffs, NJ: Prentice-Hall, 1984) and Michael L. Tushman and Elaine Romanelli, "Organizational Evolution: A Metamorphosis Model of Convergence and Reorientation," *Research in Organizational Behavior*, Vol. 7, 1985, pp. 171–222. And for a summary of some evidence related to levels of uncertainty rather than strategic change, see Hugh Courtney, Jane Kirkland, and Patrick Viguerie, "Strategy under Uncertainty," *Harvard Business Review* (November-December 1997), pp. 67–79.

41. Michael L. Tushman and Charles A. O'Reilly, "The Ambidextrous Organization: Managing Evolutionary and Revolutionary Change," *California Management Review*, Vol. 38 (Summer 1996), pp. 8–30.

42. The three bullet points that follow are all quotes excerpted from pages 26–28 of Tushman and O'Reilly, *op. cit.*

43. Andrew S. Grove, *Only the Paranoid Survive* (New York: Currency Doubleday, 1996), p. 3.

Credits

Exhibit 2.4: Reprinted with permission of Partners HealthCare Systems, Inc., "Supply Curve for Boston Hospitals." (A) ICCH # 696-062. **Exhibit 2.5:** Reprinted with permission of The Free Press, a Division of Simon & Schuster from COMPETITIVE ADVANTAGE by Michael E. Porter. Copyright © 1985 by The Free Press. **Exhibit 2.6:** Reprinted with permission of Currency Doubleday from CO-OPETITION, "The Net Value" by Adam Brandenburger and Barry Nalebuff. Copyright © 1996 by Currency Doubleday. **Exhibit 3.4:** Adapted with permission of The Free Press, a Division of Simon & Schuster from COMPETITIVE STRATEGY: Techniques for Analyzing Industries and Competitors by Michael E. Porter. Copyright © 1980, 1998 by The Free Press. **Exhibit 4.2:** Reprinted with permission of The Free Press, a Division of Simon & Schuster from COMPETITIVE STRATEGY: Porter's Generic Strategies by Michael E. Porter. Copyright © 1980 by The Free Press. **Exhibit 4.3:** Reprinted with permission of The Free Press, a Division of Simon & Schuster from COMMITMENT: The Dynamic of Strategy by Pankaj Ghemawat. Copyright © 1991 by Pankaj Ghemawat. **Exhibit 4.6:** Reprinted with permission of Stanford University Graduate School of Business from "E-Trade Securities, Inc.," by Rajiv Lal. Case No. M-286, 1996. **Exhibit 4.7:** Jeffrey H. Dyer, "Does Governance Matter?" in *Organization Science*, Vol 7, p. 6, 1996. Reprinted with permission. **Exhibit 5.1:** Reprinted by permission of *Harvard Business Review*: Southwest Airlines' Activity System, p. 73. From "What is Strategy?" by Michael E. Porter, Nov.–Dec. 1996. Copyright © 1996 by the President and Fellows of Harvard College; all rights reserved. **Exhibit 5.4:** James L. Heskett, "Establishing Strategic Direction: Aligning Elements of Strategy." Copyright © 1987 by the President and Fellows of Harvard College. Harvard Business School Case 388-033. This case was prepared by James L. Heskett under the direction of his supervisor as the basis for class discussion rather than to illustrate either effective or ineffective handling of an administrative situation. Reprinted with permission of Harvard Business School.

Name Index

Abernathy, William, 13, 14–15
Andrews, Kenneth, 5, 6, 113, 116
Ansoff, Igor, 7
Auletta, Ken, 86
Bain, Joe, 24, 54
Barnard, Chester I., 1, 3, 4
Baron, David, 35
Borch, Fred, 10, 11
Brandenburger, Adam, 21, 32, 33, 36, 58
Buffet, Warren, 19, 20
Carroll, Lewis, 83
Caves, Richard, 25
Chamberlin, Edward, 24
Chandler, Alfred D., Jr., 1, 3
Christensen, C. Roland, 5, 127
Christensen, Clayton M., 95
Clausewitz, Carl von, 2
Coase, Ronald, 4
Commons, John, 4
Cournot, Antoine, 24
Dell, Michael, 60
Drucker, Peter, 3
Dyer, Jeffrey, 96
Einstein, Albert, 36
Emerson, Ralph Waldo, 49
Ford, Henry, 13
Foster, Richard, 83
Fruhan, William E., Jr., 82–83
Gary, Judge, 27
Ghemawat, Pankaj, 82, 83, 128
Gluck, Fred, 14
Graddy, Elizabeth, 42
Grove, Andy, 33, 111, 130–131
Hall, William, 54–55
Hayes, Robert, 14–15
Henderson, Bruce, 8, 9, 13
Hunt, Michael, 51
Jensen, Michael, 104

Kennedy, Robert, 85
Klepper, Steven, 42
Lenin, Vladimir Ilyich, 4
Levitt, Theodore, 7
Lewis, Walker, 53
Marshall, Alfred, 22
Mason, Edward S., 24
Morgenstern, Oskar, 3, 76
Murphy, Kevin, 104
Nalebuff, Barry, 21, 32, 33, 36
Neumann, John von, 3, 76
O'Reilly, Charles A., 128–129
Penrose, Edith, 4–5
Perot, H. Ross, 102
Pisano, Gary, 124
Porter, Michael, 21, 25, 35, 54–55, 56, 80–81, 113–115
Ricart i Costa, Joan, 128
Robinson, Joan, 24
Schelling, Thomas C., 1
Schumpeter, Joseph, 4, 90
Selznick, Philip, 4, 80
Shuen, Amy, 124
Sloan, Alfred, 3, 5, 13
Smale, John, 105
Smith, Adam, 2, 3
Smith, George Albert, Jr., 5
Stuart, Gus, 58
Sutton, John, 42–43
Teece, David, 124
Tilles, Seymour, 9
Townsend, Robert, 121
Tushman, Michael L., 128–129
Wayne, Kenneth, 13
Wernerfelt, Birger, 116
Whitehead, Alfred North, 75
Williams, Jeffrey, 90
Williamson, Oliver, 103

Company Index

ABC, 85
CBS, 85
NBC, 85
American Safety Razor, 121
Anheuser-Busch, 42
Arthur D. Little, 12
Asea Brown Boveri (ABB), 129
Avis, 58
Bain & Company, 52, 54
Black and Decker, 9
Boston Consulting Group (BCG), 8–10, 93
Brigham and Women's Hospital, 23–24
Calyx and Corolla, 66
Canon, 126
Carmike, 86
Charles Schwab, 91–92, 94
Chrysler Corporation, 96, 97, 100, 103
Circus Circus, 69–70
Coca-Cola, 59, 60
Continental Lite, 115
Crown Cork & Seal, 29, 99
Edward Jones, 71
Enterprise Rent-a-Car, 58
Ernst & Young, 93
E*Trade, 91–92
Fiat, 66
Fisher Body, 98
Ford Motor Company, 3, 96, 103
Fox, 85
Gannett, 126
General Electric (GE), 8, 10–11
General Motors (GM), 3, 31, 33, 96, 98,
    102–103, 105
Gillette, 112, 120–123, 125–126
Goldman, Sachs, 57–58
Haagen Dazs, 58
Harvard Medical Center (HMC), 23–24
Hertz, 58
Hewlett-Packard, 129
Holland Sweetener Company (HSC), 59–60,
    79, 85
Hostess, 61, 62–63, 67, 69

Hyundai, 55
IBM, 70
Intel, 32–33, 94, 100, 112, 130–131
International Dairy Queen, 58
Johnson & Johnson, 129
Levi Strauss, 68
Little Debbie, 61, 63, 67, 69
Liz Claiborne, 60–61
McDonald's, 56
McKinsey & Company, 13, 14, 15, 54, 93
Marks and Spencer, 57
Massachusetts General Hospital, 23–24
Merrill Lynch, 58, 71, 92–93
Microsoft Corporation, 32–33, 100, 126
Miller, 42
Morgan Stanley, 58
New Balance, 66
Nike, 66
Nintendo, 33, 44, 88
Nordstrom, 66
Nucor, 49
NutraSweet, 59, 79
Ontario Baking, 63, 67
Pepsi-Cola, 59, 60
Prudential Securities, 92
Quantum, 94
Savory Pastries, 63, 67, 69
Schick, 121
Southwest Airlines, 70, 112, 113, 114–115, 116–119
Strategic Planning Associates, 52, 53
Texas Instruments, 9
Toyota, 55, 96
United Auto Workers (UAW), 98, 103
U.S. Air Force, 4
U.S. Army, 4
U.S. Marine Corps, 4
U.S. Navy, 4
United States Steel, 27
United Steel Workers, 31
Wal-Mart, 6
Wilkinson, 121
Yahoo!, 69

Subject Index

Activity-system view, 112–116
   tresource-based view versus, 112–113
Adaptation, to business landscape, 43
Added value, 58–60, 84–95
   holdup as threat to appropriability of, 95–101
   imitation as threat to, 84–90
   slack as threat to appropriability of, 101–105
   substitution as threat to, 84, 90–95
Asset-specificity, reducing, as remedy for
    holdup, 99
Automobile industry
   complementors and, 33
   holdup in, 96–100
   supplier power in, 31
Bargaining
   hard, as remedy for holdup, 99
   unrestricted, 59
Bargaining power, as remedy for holdup, 98–99
Behavioral theory, 79–81
Benchmarking, 103
"Best alternative to a negotiated agreement"
    (BATNA), 98–99
Bonding resources, managing slack and, 104–105
Boundaries, for mapping business landscapes,
    35–38
Brewing industry, mapping relationships and,
    40, 42
Business models, 19–20
Business schools, founding of, 5
Buyer power, 30–31
Capabilities, dynamic theories and, 120, 124–127
Change
   activity-system view and, 115–116
   challenge of, 127–131
   mobilizing for, managing slack and, 105
Choices, integrated, 70–71
Commitments, dynamic theories and, 120–124
Competence, distinctive, 7
Competition
   competitor analysis and, 80–81
   degree of rivalry and, 25, 27–28
   oligopolistic, 24
Competitive advantage, 49–72

added value and, 58–60
choice and, 71
cost analysis and, 52–53
cost vs. differentiation and, 54–58
differentiation analysis and, 53–54
dual, 56
evolution of, 82
internal fit and, 70–71
positioning analysis and. *See* Positioning
    analysis
Competitive relationships, mapping of, 39–40
Complementarities
   activity-system view and, 115
   boundaries for mapping business landscapes
    and, 36
Complementors, 32–34
Complexity, as barrier to imitation, 89
Computer hardware/software industries, 32–33
Concentration, relative, complementors and, 33
Contracts
   as barrier to imitation, 87
   as remedy for holdup, 97–98
Cooperative relationships, mapping of, 39–40
Cospecialization, holdup stemming from, 95–101
Cost drivers, 52–53, 63, 64, 65
Costs
   analysis of, 52–53, 62–65
   differentiation versus, 54–58
Cybertrading, 90–93
Demand, price-elasticity of, 22
Differentiation
   analysis of, 53–54
   costs versus, 54–58
   horizontal and vertical, 68
Discount brokers, 90–93
Distinctive competence, 7
Dual competitive advantage, 56
Dynamic efficiency, 128
Dynamic theories, 119–127
   capabilities and, 120, 124–127
   commitments and, 120–124
Dynamic thinking, mapping relationships and,
    40–43

Economies of scale and scope, as barrier to imitation, 86
Efficiency, dynamic and static, 128–129
Endogenous sunk costs, 42–43
Entry, threat of, 28–29
Entry barriers, 28–29
Equilibrium
    for games, 77
    punctuated, 128
Evolutionary dynamics, 81–83
Exogenous sunk costs, 42–43
Experience curve, 9
Field maps, 53
Fighting, as response to substitution, 94
"Five forces" framework, 24–31
    buyer power and, 30–31
    degree of rivalry and, 25, 27–28
    supplier power and, 31
    threat of entry and, 28–29
    threat of substitutes and, 29–30
"Focus" option, 55
Free cash flow, 104–105
Freewheeling games, 76
Game theory, 76–79
"Generic" strategies, 55–58
Geographic scope, boundaries for mapping business landscapes and, 38
Governance, changing, managing slack and, 105
Harvard Business School, 5
Harvard School, 24
Harvesting, as response to substitution, 95
Holdup, as threat to value appropriation, 95–101
Horizontal differentiation, 68
Horizontal scope, boundaries for mapping business landscapes and, 37
Imitation, as threat to added value, 84–90
Industrial organization (IO), 24–25
Industrial Revolutions, 2–3
Information
    gathering of, managing slack and, 103
    private, as barrier to imitation, 87
Integration
    asymmetric, complementors and, 34
    as remedy for holdup, 98
Internal consistency, 56–57
Internal fit, 70–71
Interorganizational relationships, 98
Korean War, 4

Landscape analysis, 19–46
    adapting to/shaping business landscape and, 43–44
    drawing boundaries for, 35–38
    "five forces" framework and, 24–31
    mapping key relationships and, 38–43
    supply-demand analysis and, 21–24
    value net and, 32–34
Learning, as barrier to imitation, 87
Learning curves, 3
Learn-to-burn ratios, 123–124
Lock-in, 121
Lock-out, 121–122
Mapping business landscapes. See Landscape analysis
Market segmentation, 68
Market share, complementors and, 34
Mass customization, 68
Modular activity systems, 116
Monitoring behavior, managing slack and, 103–104
Moral suasion, 104
Network externalities, as barrier to imitation, 87–88
Nonmarket relationships, 34–35
Non-zero-sum games, 76
Norms, managing slack and, 104
Not responding, as response to substitution, 93
Oligopolistic competition, 24
Online stock trading, 90–93
Opportunity costs, 63
Payoff matrix, 76–78
Performance incentives, managing slack and, 104
Pharmaceutical industry
    buyer power in, 30–31
    degree of rivalry in, 27
    entry barriers in, 28
    substitutes and, 29
    supplier power in, 31
Portfolio analysis, 9–15
    problems with, 13–15
    strategic business units and, 10–13
Positioning analysis, 60–70
    analyzing relative costs and, 62–65
    analyzing relative willingness to pay and, 65–68
    exploring strategic options and making choices and, 68–70

Price-elasticity of demand, 22
Private information, as barrier to imitation, 87
Professional management, 3
Profitability Optimization Model (PROM), 8
Profit Impact of Market Strategies (PIMS)
        program, 11–12
Pull-through, complementors and, 34
Punctuated equilibria, 128
Reaction functions, 78
Recombining, as response to substitution, 94
Red Queen effect, 83
Relationships
    as barrier to imitation, 87
    building, as remedy for holdup, 99–100
Resource-based view, 116–119
    activity-system view versus, 112–113
Resources, 65
    bonding, managing slack and, 104–105
Retaliation, threats of, as barrier to imitation,
        88–89
Rivalry, degree of, 25, 27–28
Rugged landscape, 70–71
Rule-based games, 76
Scale, economies of, as barrier to imitation, 86
Scope, 53
    boundaries for mapping business landscapes
        and, 37–38
    economies of, as barrier to imitation, 87
Segmentation, 68
Self-enforcement, 87
Sensitivity analysis, 64–65
Shaping, of business landscape, 43–44
Slack, as threat to value appropriation,
        101–105
Standard Industrial Classification (SIC) code, 36
Static efficiency, 128
Steel industry
    buyer power in, 30, 31
    degree of rivalry in, 27
    entry barriers in, 28–29
    substitutes and, 29–30
    supplier power in, 31
Stock trading, online, 90–93
Straddling, as response to substitution, 94–95
Strategic business units (SBUs), portfolio analysis
        and, 10–13

Strategic groups, 49
Strategic inflection points, 130–131
Strategy, 1–16
    academic underpinnings of, 4–8
    background of, 2–4
    defined, 1
    exploring strategic options and making
        choices and, 68–70
    "generic," 55–58
    rise of consultants on, 8–13
Substitution
    boundaries for mapping business landscapes
        and, 36
    threat of, 29–30
    as threat to added value, 84, 90–95
Sunk costs, exogenous and endogenous, 42–43
Supplier power, 31
Supply-demand analysis, 21–24
Switching
    costs of, complementors and, 33
    as response to substitution, 94
SWOT framework, 5–7
Television networks, imitation by, 85
Third-party enforcement, 87
Time lags, as barrier to imitation, 89
Trade-offs
    activity-system view and, 115
    between cost and differentiation, 56, 57
Trust, development of, as remedy for holdup,
        100–101
Unbundling, complementors and, 34
Unrestricted bargaining, 59
Upgrading, as barrier to imitation, 89–90
Value, 58–60
    added. *See* Added value
Value chain, 54, 61, 65
Value Line classification system, 35–36
Value net, 32–34
Vertical chains, 58–60
Vertical differentiation, 68
Vertical scope, boundaries for mapping business
        landscapes and, 37
Wharton School, 5
Willingness to pay, analysis of, 65–68
World War II, 3–4
Zero-sum games, 76